★ ★ ★ ★ ★
BOOT CAMP
→ FOR ←
FINANCIAL
ADVISORS

DAVID CLEMENKO

CONTENTS

Dedication

This book is dedicated to my Poppy.

It was my Poppy who I first saw in front of an audience. It was my Poppy to whom I owe my ability to share my thoughts and passion through verbal presentations. And it was my Poppy who loved me as only a grandfather could.

Take a journey with David as he shares what he has learned in his eleven years as a coach and trainer to more than 10,000 financial advisors at the world's largest financial firm. In the span of four years as the National Marketing Trainer for their Global Wealth Management Division, David traveled to more than 350 Merrill Lynch offices in 43 states. Now this former U.S. Marine Drill Instructor puts his unique combination of discipline, business savvy and marketing expertise to work to help you take your business to new levels. You will get back to basics, implement new processes and put structure around everything you do. David's unique techniques for building a marketing plan for prospecting and a contact strategy for relationships are simple, strategic and actionable. This book will take you through my Nine Prospecting Methods with best practices that you can put to work today. If you are ready to grow and transform your business, this is a MUST READ.

Wall Street Warfighters Foundation

A portion of every book sale will be donated to one of the organizations nearest and dearest to David's heart. The Wall Street Warfighters Foundation is a 501(c)(3) nonprofit organization dedicated to helping wounded veterans transition back into the workforce by training them for careers in the financial services industry.

FOREWORD

by Peter E. Eckerline, CRPC®, CFM
Managing Director-Investments
Wealth Management Advisor
Merrill Lynch Wealth Management

I've had a lot of success in my nearly three decades in the financial services industry.

I'm a partner in a very productive Merrill Lynch Wealth Management team. I've been ranked five times by the *Twin Cities Business Journal* as Minnesota's no. 1 Wealth Advisor, made the *Barron's* Top 100 list, and was named by *Minnesota Law and Politics* as one of the state's most trusted financial advisors.

So you can probably imagine my reaction when David Clemenko—a person I had never met or heard of—burst into my office about five years ago and challenged me to do better. While on one hand, I was thinking there really wasn't much *anyone* could teach me at this stage of my career, on the other hand, David's message almost instantly began to penetrate my "who-do-you-think-you-are" filter.

I've always prided myself on staying a step ahead of the competition through superior marketing. But David has helped me move three steps ahead. For example, while I've never been hesitant to cold call—a strategy that helped me build a business—David showed me how to mine the data I gained. Suddenly, every call offered tremendous value.

David also worked to help me expand and better define my value proposition, which gave me an enhanced method for illustrating my real worth to top-tier prospects and clients. And he helped me create customized literature that goes a long, long way in differentiating me and my team from our competitors.

While I'm sorry to see David leave Merrill Lynch, it's comforting to know he is still just a phone call away. Because he and I constantly brainstorm by phone, he will continue to play a role in my marketing efforts. And if you're motivated to improve your positioning and revenue, you should find a way to make him a part of your marketing team, too.

CHAPTER 1

BRAIDS AND BOWS

I was a damned good marine drill instructor. I was also a single dad, living just outside of Parris Island, South Carolina, with my children, five-year-old Brittany and three-year-old Michael.

Brittany, a gorgeous little blonde with eyes that could turn the coldest heart to mush, had been born in Honolulu, Hawaii. Her beautiful round face, framed by platinum blond hair, never failed to attract native Hawaiians to her delightfully cabbage patch look-alike features. Michael, the personality of the family, could charm the pants off anyone. He had sympathetic hazel eyes and a soft demeanor that could instantly put you at his command and render you defenseless.

Both kids were devastated by the separation. To leave their mother and everything with which they were comfortable, was unthinkable. I used to lie in bed and wonder what must be going through their young minds. What conclusions have they drawn? What do they think happened? Who did they blame? Me? Their mother? Themselves? Minutes would turn into hours until, exhausted, I would carry them from their rooms into my bed and just hold them.

"This is not the life I intended for you," I whispered to both on hundreds of such occasions. "I'm so sorry for what's happened to you." Those nights were, perhaps, the worst I've ever experienced, and they would drag on for well over a year before I was able to let them go.

And then suddenly came my personal epiphany.

It was pretty much a routine day—other than the exchange I would have with my daughter that would change my life! The three of us were sitting at the kitchen table. We had just finished dinner, which consisted of fish sticks and Ore-Ida French Fries (the only thing I knew how to cook), and I was helping Brittany with her homework while Michael was coloring.

Brittany looked up at me and dropped a bombshell. "Daddy, why doesn't my hair look like the other girls'? Why can't I have ponytails and braids like the other girls do?"

I had no idea what to say. In two sentences—maybe five seconds—she had summarized what had been haunting me every night since the divorce. All I ever wanted since I was very young was to have a normal family. My dream was a loving wife, healthy children, house with a picket fence, doting dog, warm fireplace, and happy family dinners. That's what I expected but missed out on.

I sat at my dinette table, forced to realize that for the rest of my children's lives they would not have a normal family. Divorce was the ultimate failure for a person whose dream was to be a family man. To me, it's the equivalent of someone who dreams of being a doctor but somehow kills a patient and loses his or her license to practice medicine.

I couldn't think of an answer for my daughter other than "Baby, Daddy doesn't know how to do that." Brilliant, huh? My daughter was looking for parental wisdom and guidance, and my answer was, basically, "Duh." I felt like a complete failure and jackass.

Brittany looked at me for a long moment, her silence deafening and her eyes piercing. After an eternity (just a couple of seconds, but it seemed at the time to be *forever*), she said nothing and went back to her schoolwork. Actually, she didn't have to say anything because her look said it all. Her expression said, clearly, "That's just not good enough."

She was right. It was time to stop feeling sorry for myself and the broken family I had helped create. It was time to start shaping the family life I wanted with the tools I was given. The next day, I went to a bookstore, but I was too embarrassed to ask for help in finding a book about ponytails. (I wasn't even sure there was such a thing).

I spent at least an hour in the kids' section, then meandered off to the self-help section. After what seemed like hours, there it was, a spiral-bound book that seemed to jump out at me, titled *Braids and Bows*. I wondered if this was how Moses felt when he received the Ten Commandments; that's how overwhelmed I was as I flipped through the pages.

I had no idea there were so many ways to braid hair, so many ponytails, so many pins and flashy ribbons. *Yikes!* It gave me a new respect for the time it must take to master this unfamiliar art form. But just like a new arrival at Parris Island, I needed the basics. I had to walk before I could fly.

I bought the book and experimented for weeks before I felt I understood the art of the ponytail. But I got it, and that made me realize I had spent an enormous amount of time and energy coming up with excuses about why I couldn't do things. Instead of directing my attention to knocking down the barriers and walls that were standing in front of me, I was making excuses for myself.

I knew then that I could accomplish anything life was going to put before me, and I was going to be the best dad—and mom—my kids could ever imagine. Would there be setbacks? Sure. I'm human, and I've made mistakes—plenty! But never again would I use the excuse "I don't know or I can't."

The question I'm asking you (actually, it's the question you need to ask yourself) is "How bad do you want it?"

As a financial advisor (FA), you have an opportunity to build your business and inspire those around you. You need to throw away excuses about needing more time, more money, fewer compliance restraints, or not enough home-office support. Start looking at those excuses as miniwalls you must break through every day because, each time you do, you bring yourself one step closer to success.

I created my own walls by thinking the perfect family life had to be a mom, dad, and a house with a picket fence. Certainly that might have been ideal, but I can provide a great life for my children no matter what.

More than a decade later, *Braids and Bows* still sits by my bedside as a reminder of the day I discovered I could accomplish whatever I put my mind to. As you continue through this book, remember what drew you to it in the first place; remember that it's all about believing in yourself as a financial advisor.

The more you believe in your own abilities, the more your clients will be inspired by you and put their trust in you. The world has changed, but the trust between clients and advisors has intensified. Clients want to feel safe in an unsafe world. They need to believe that you have their best interests in mind with everything you do. Get out of bed every day with your clients' best interests at heart, and success will certainly follow you.

*   *   *

On a side note, if this story happened to leave you wondering what happens when you combine a hairdresser with a Marine Corps drill instructor, you would end up with a very disciplined, very tight, and very straight ponytail! For the guys reading this book, a little piece of advice I learned the hard way: when you grab the ponytail in two pieces and pull those pieces apart to tighten them up, it hurts. Since I never had hair long enough for a ponytail, I didn't have an appreciation for what that might feel like. It would take a crying little girl, multiple times, to enlighten this wannabe mommy.

CHAPTER 2

YOUR WILLINGNESS TO CHANGE IS YOUR BEST STRATEGY FOR SUCCESS

Having the ability to shift strategy, adjust sail, and accept change was a painful lesson for me. I always thought it was the things around me that changed, but as Thoreau said, "Things do not change, we change." It didn't take me long to find out how right he was.

As I traveled across the country speaking to financial advisors in the wake of the collapse on Wall Street, one thing was painfully clear. Many FAs had no idea how to adapt to the changing atmosphere.

My company—the mighty Merrill Lynch—was brought to its knees by the financial crisis. The swagger that had always been so much a part of the famed *thundering herd*—the aggressive financial advisors who had vaulted Merrill to the top and kept it there for nearly a century—seemed to be drifting away right before my eyes.

It was sad because I had fallen in love with Mother Merrill, a company very similar to my beloved Marine Corps with a culture of excellence and esprit de corps. To watch the dismantling of a company that had for so long served its clients with trust and dignity, was unbearable. During this unfathomable period, my job was to help FAs market themselves to disbelieving prospects and increasingly tenuous clients.

The marketplace was telling even the mightiest financial advisors that the old way of doing business was not going to work anymore. If they were going to continue to be successful, they needed to change their old way of thinking. Somehow, I had to inspire them to recapture their glory days by embracing change. But what, I asked myself, did I really know about change?

It was 1996. I was a drill instructor with Third Battalion, Kilo Company, at the famed Parris Island Marine Base. The sign that greets all visitors leaves no doubt what the mission has been for over one hundred years (and will be for the next one hundred and the one hundred after that):

Parris Island—Where We Make Marines.

No matter who you are or what you do, everyone at Parris Island is there to support that singular mission. Being a drill instructor had been the hardest job I ever had but, without a doubt, the most rewarding.

What a responsibility it is to motivate, mentor, and inspire young men to become what I believe is America's finest fighting force. My mission was clear, my focus certain, and my strategy straightforward: make marines. An unambiguous mission statement if ever there was one.

During my tenure on the island, I made over two hundred U.S. Marines, and on my last check, they were all still alive and many continue playing a role in America's defense. As a drill instructor, it's my job to lay the foundation because the stronger the foundation, the more successful the marine.

Just as I was becoming comfortable in my drill instructor role, life threw me that curveball I talked about in chapter 1 and rocked my world. One day I was shaping recruits, and the next day I was on my way to North Carolina to collect my two small children. I turned from being a feared drill instructor into Mr. Mom. I now had the lives of a three- and five-year-old in my hands. While I did have family, they were twelve hours away in New Jersey. They did what they could to help, but ultimately, I was on my own for the day-to-day child-raising duties.

How did I deal with it? I immediately tried to do what I see financial advisors doing today: I tried to force the same strategy that worked so well for making marines into this new job of taking care of two small children. I found out very quickly it didn't work that way, and I remember the exact day and circumstances that I learned this lesson.

My son was three years old, and it was time for potty training. How did I know it was time? Well, it didn't come from Dr. Spock or a pop psychology magazine article. I knew it was time because I didn't like changing diapers, and I hated how much the diapers cost me.

I remember the night like it was yesterday. I was cleaning up dinner—a healthy portion of fish sticks and apple sauce—and I looked at my son with the same voice and body language I used with my marine recruits. I pointed my finger in his face and said, "Let me tell you something, young man, you are going to use the potty, and you are going to do it *right now*"!

My son looked at me intently and, after a slight pause, burst out laughing. *Are you kidding me?* I thought he would cower, cry, be intimidated, and say, "Yes, Daddy." I thought he would run to the potty and do what I told him to do, and then I would move on to the next challenges with my drill instructor strategy intact.

I often thought about the talks I would have with all the moms at day care and my family members at home. "Look," I would tell them, "I did it in two minutes. I potty-trained my son in 120 seconds!" Everyone told me how hard it would be, but none of them were drill instructors versed in Marine Corps methods and tactics. Vindication would be mine.

Unfortunately, it didn't quite happen that way. When my son laughed at me—deep, from-the-belly laughter—I was completely confused. I thought he would respond so differently, and I couldn't fathom how I could be so wrong. I was a menacing drill instructor who made grown men shake when I approached them. How in God's good name could this toddler, this tiny little three-feet-high child, think I was funny?

But that's what he said: "Daddy, you're so funny." Funny? There was nothing funny about it. But I quickly realized that the same time-honored methods, strategies, and tactics that worked so well for making marines

at Parris Island was not going to work here. To be successful, I would
need to adjust my strategy to conform to the changes that were taking
place all around me. The mission had changed, and I had to adapt to the
change.

As a financial advisor, you too must change with and adapt to the world
around you. I wish I could tell you that the world is the same, that
clients haven't changed, that everyone trusts brokerage firms, financial
advisors, and Wall Street just as they did four or five years ago. But
that's just not so. We all know it's different and that you have to work
harder to get the business that seemed to come so much easier not that
long ago. In the new financial environment, you too must change, shift,
and refocus on the basics.

As the greatest generation fades, the mighty boomers fill the marketplace
with their own ideals, thoughts, cultures, and vision for how they want
to retire. Right behind is Generation X: how will they frame retirement
and what will the world look like when it's their turn? Will you still be
the same financial advisor their grandfather had, or will you embrace
the changing world around you?

Since the recent crash on Wall Street and after meeting thousands of
advisors across the country, I've divided them into three categories:

Business as Usual
These are usually very seasoned FAs, men and women who
have been doing business for over ten years. Most started their
practices through cold calling and seminars, and they've been
exceptionally successful. Once they achieved a base book
of business, they quickly moved to what I call a 2P—two
prospecting methods of networking and referrals.

Those are two of the nine successful prospecting methods, all of
which I'll cover in another chapter. But for now, it's important
to understand that recently the business-as-usual FAs have had
trouble finding success by just using these two methods. When
I probe this category of FAs and ask what their primary goal is,
they almost always say, "I want to grow." The problem is that
they are only willing to use networking and referrals as their

way to achieve growth even though those two methods are not currently increasing their pipeline.

Yes, networking and referrals are extremely powerful methods for building a business, but they require a huge amount of time and trust. And how can you grow your book of business using only two methods that are not producing the results you're seeking? This business-as-usual group is unwilling to turn to other methods of prospecting. Many of them feel as if they're taking two steps back in their careers, or they believe they're just too good, too sophisticated, to make cold calls—or even to run a seminar because it's a crap shoot as to whether the event might be filled with plate lickers (those who come just for the food) or millionaires, and what a waste of their precious time.

This is a group I cannot help because my methods are constructed around changing the norm, shifting and refocusing strategies. If you fall into this group and you truly want to grow, may I suggest you open your mind and move to the next category?

Stuck in the Middle
This group is not as difficult to deal with as the business-as-usual crowd. This group includes every type of financial advisor on the street: old and new to the business, seasoned and young, portfolio managers, relationship builders, stock pickers, analysts, and every combination you can imagine.

This is a group that understands the world has changed, and they totally get that their businesses aren't growing. These FAs want to grow but have no idea where to begin. They make changes on the fly, hoping each attempt holds the magic recipe to success but, ultimately, don't see the gains they're wishing for. They are generally willing to change, but at the same time, they're cautious.

If you fall into this group, this book is going to be exactly what you need. It will help you get back to basics, adjust your strategy and focus, and go at this business of growth with a new energy and outlook matched only by the successes in our business!

Ahead of the Game

These are usually the most successful financial advisors in the building. They understand that having a tunnel vision, getting caught in a rut, and being complacent can be deadly to business. They've already changed and adjusted. They constantly go back to the nine prospecting methods (you'll learn about them in chapter 5) to add, subtract, and modify what is working and what isn't.

Every year, I go to the Midwest to work with many different advisors and teams. On one occasion, my schedule had me in Minnesota in February, which was the last time I would visit that area in the winter! I had never experienced twenty-two degrees below zero, and I have no interest in doing so again. I had felt severe cold during my marine duties, but twenty-two below is just ridiculous.

Anyway, I ran into a very impressive team in the Midwest, which was anchored by a very successful personality who is listed virtually every year as one of *Barron's* Top 100 FAs. When I first met him, he told me he loved hearing that FAs were hiring interns to make cold calls for them. Why did he like hearing that?

"David," he said, "when FAs hire people to do cold calls for them, I know I'm way ahead of them. I still make all my own cold calls, and I don't mind a bit." What a powerful response. Even though this financial advisor was incredibly successful, he still wanted to grow. He knew that to do so, he would have to continue to reinvent himself so he and his team would not get complacent or stagnant. He knew that he could certainly outsell novices, so he made cold calls himself.

If you fall into this category, this book will be a huge help as you continue to redefine yourself, your team, and your business.

If you are still not convinced about the immediate need for change, contemplate this: when you close your eyes and think about companies such as Goldman Sachs, Merrill Lynch, Citi, Morgan Stanley, Smith

Barney, and UBS, what comes to mind? Think about where you were in 2005/6, where we were as a society, and what was happening with Wall Street. If I asked you that same question five years ago, would your answer have been different? More importantly, do you think your clients' and prospects' answers would be different *today*?

If you answered yes, then you believe that the trust and perception of financial firms, the markets, Wall Street, and financial advisors have changed—and not for the better. And that means you must change as well. You must shift and adjust as events and opportunities around you continue to change. You need to understand that you must be able to explain to your clients why they should do business with you, trust you, and give you their life savings *now*. You can no longer rest solely on your brand or your company to do the job for you. The relationship is yours to gain or lose.

My belief is that by the end of this book, you will be a 4 or 5P, using four or five of the nine prospecting methods. When that happens, you will see your brand awareness expand, your pipeline explode, and your business grow.

CHAPTER 3

LEAD YOUR CLIENTS, COMMUNICATE WITH YOUR CLIENTS

(It's not much different than leading and making marines.)

Some people are born with the gift of leadership while others have to be taught. However you acquire your leadership skills, you don't have to be a general or a CEO to make an impact; you just need to be truly willing to put your clients' interests first. The clients are the heartbeat of your organization, and you will find that communication is your best defense for retaining those clients.

Not everyone understands the transformative effect a great leader can have on someone's life, and what it can mean to your clients and your book of business. During the collapse of Wall Street in 2008, one of the biggest problems we had to overcome was getting advisors to communicate with their clients, ensure them that their money was safe, that things were going to be all right. You will find that the absence of communication leads to chaos, and that leads to unhappy and unfaithful clients. Just like a general on the battlefield, you need to instill confidence, compassion, and control in every situation you find yourself in when it comes to your business. Follow my journey through the U.S. Marine Corps to fully grasp what leadership and communication can do for your practice.

It was 1996, and I was stationed in Camp Lejeune, North Carolina. We lived in a three-bedroom ranch in the town of Jacksonville, the armpit of the east. Riddled with pawnshops, tattoo parlors, seedy bars, and strip clubs, it had the stench of a saloon at 4:00 a.m. It was to be my home for almost three years and a place that I have no interest in visiting for the rest of my life.

I was the platoon sergeant for what was basically a technical group of marines: photographers, videographers, and graphic artists. I was the motivator, the guy who pumped them up and excited them about being marines. I held inspections, training exercises, motivational runs, and an occasional surprise team-building event. There were mornings when my marines warily asked, "How far we going to run today, Sergeant C?" And I would flash a smile and say, "Not today, boys. Today we're going to have a little fun." My "fun" exercises consisted of water polo, soccer, football, and even kickball. My mission was to motivate the troops, and I did a damned good job . . . even though I made about a million mistakes along the way. The basic principles I lived by was to ensure that (1) the mission was being accomplished, and (2) the marines were always taken care of. When I kept my principles at the top, everything worked no matter what mistakes I made.

There comes a time, around the sixth or seventh year, in every enlisted marine's career, that you have to make a move to a job you may not like or want. If you want to get promoted and retire with twenty or more years, you must serve in what is called a "B" Billet, also known as a secondary assignment. You have two choices, and even today, I'm still not sure which is the shorter straw. You can either become a drill instructor, making marines in Parris Island or San Diego, or you can become a recruiter and beg young seventeen- and eighteen-year-old kids to sign the dotted line while fighting a suspicious and terrified Mom and Dad. If you decide not to make a decision, it will be made for you. Being the control freak that I am, I thought it best to make that decision myself.

If you haven't figured it out yet, you'll soon realize that my personality is that of an extroverted salesman (a God-given talent, as I see it—and in the family genes, thanks to my Poppy). Logic would say that recruiting would have been my best choice. But this isn't logic. It's life, and life has a funny way of steamrolling logic. So I chose the drill instructor route because taking the DI job was about being able to control my future and career. As a recruiter, I thought even if I were the best salesman in the world, what if kids just didn't want to join?

What if I was busting my hump, making my calls, visiting schools, and I was assigned to an area full of kids with no ambition, who just wanted a life in the college dorms; how do you compete with that? I just figured that a big part of the recruiting job was out of my control and I *love* being in control. Instead of having to kiss the rear end of an eighteen-year-old recruit, I had the opportunity to kick their rear ends in Parris Island. Easy choice.

This is a life lesson: understand what you can control, especially when it can decide the success of your career. It's the same lesson financial advisors need to learn. In the next chapter, you'll see that you have two avenues for building better, deeper, and more longer-lasting relationships with your clients. The first is through the performance of the portfolio. There is no faster way to build loyalty and trust than through good performance. In Wall Street's heyday, a good portfolio took care of most of the heavy relationship lifting.

The second avenue is through the hundreds of opportunities, large and small, you have to build deeper understandings and connections with people. This requires more work and takes longer than the portfolio route. But which is better? The problem with performance is that it's not 100 percent controlled by the FA. Case in point is what happened in 2008 to FAs who hadn't taken the time to get to know their clients'. They didn't listen to what their hopes, dreams, and fears were. They didn't know the names of their children, grandchildren or any personal information that might lead to a deeper relationship with the client. When the market crashed, what incentive did those clients have to stay with their advisors? The FAs had built loyalty and trust through performance—but they couldn't sustain it because they couldn't control it.

Going down the more difficult path requires a much larger commitment from you, but it is the more rational avenue because you can control the outcome. You decide how deep you want to take the relationship. Will you take the time to look for opportunities and capitalize on them, or do you want to take the quick route over which you have less control? In my case, I brought my personality to the drill field and tried not to lose sight of who I was, which made for some funny moments with the recruits. Well, funny for me, but not so funny for them.

I was sent to one of the hardest training schools in the Marine Corps, the Drill Instructor School in Parris Island, South Carolina. Picture a drill instructor, a mean, nasty, hard-nosed, nail-eating SOB, the kind you see in commercials and Hollywood hits. Do you know where Hollywood gets the consultants to help make cinematic DIs seem real? You bet. Parris Island, otherwise known as *hell*, and those DIs are not human.

This is what was waiting for me and eighty other marines as we awoke for our first day of Drill Instructor School. Standing at attention, I asked myself the same question as when I entered marine boot camp seven years earlier: "What the hell am I doing here?" But I knew I had to make a go of it because my career was on the line. If you failed, you were done. You couldn't be promoted; your career was over.

The school lasted three months, and I missed my children very much. I only had one opportunity during that three-month period to see them. This was very hard for me because I had not been separated from them for a long period of time since their birth. I was lucky when compared to other marines who were deployed all the time. I'm not sure if I would have stayed in the Marine Corps if I had to have been away from my children, because I knew from a very young age what kind of dad I wanted to be.

One of the most important things I wanted as a father was to be there for my kids whenever they needed me. My dad was great, but I lived in a house also ravaged by divorce. My father was a weekend warrior, a part-time father who could not be there day-to-day. I wanted to be involved in everything with my kids—from coaching sports to being on the board of directors at their nursery school to chaperoning class trips. I was the one to drop them off at school, take them to the doctor when they were sick, and put them to bed every night. So to be away from them for so long was a huge adjustment for all of us.

DI school was hard but not impossible. We yelled at the trees a lot and ran about a million miles a day. I took it all with a grain of salt and tried not to get caught up in the fanaticism. I made two great friends during this experience (one of whom became my best man when I later married the love of my life), and we were known as the Three Musketeers (how original). Gravett, McDonald, and Clemenko, a very odd group as we couldn't have been more different.

Gravett was a little guy but the oldest of the three and had a great Bob Newhart dry sense of humor (if you're too young to know who Bob Newhart is, you owe it to yourself to check him out). McDonald might have been the youngest in the entire class, but he was certainly not the weakest. He was good-looking, smart, and very capable, with country charm and a calming demeanor. Then there was me, type A, full of energy and excitement, and totally undisciplined for a guy who planned to be a drill instructor. I laughed all the time and became an expert floor waxer, the standard punishment for the rebels.

We were definitely an odd bunch, and our relaxed approach to everything in school would really piss off the GI Joe types. We knew we weren't going to be first in the class, but we were definitely not going to be last. There were the GI Joe wannabes in the top ten and a number of dumber-than-rocks marines who settled at the bottom. We were perfectly content in the middle of the class. One morning, we heard there would be a surprise inspection. *Oh great, another freaking surprise inspection.* This wasn't my strong suit because inspections required considerable attention to detail about the appearance of a uniform. *Who really cares if I have a little piece of yarn coming out of the inside of my belt loop? Really, sir, don't we have other things to pay attention to?*

During this particular inspection, Gravett was our squad leader. One of the nastiest of all the instructors stood before Gravett to get the inspection report. He was short, swarthy, and a real mean son of a bitch gunnery sergeant. Gravett was so nervous as he began his sword salute, that he lost control, and the sword flew up in the air. It was like a movie moment: time stood still as everyone's eyes followed the sword back to earth as it barely missed the sergeant and hit the ground.

I couldn't keep my composure (in marine terminology, military bearing), and I laughed so hard I was kicked out of formation and banished to clean the classroom, again. McDonald wasn't far behind, and it was good to have company while stripping, waxing, and buffing the floor for the next couple hours. This wouldn't be the last time we got into trouble. We just had a way of pissing off the instructors and GI Joes. We weren't trying to be cavalier about the training; we just decided we weren't going to take it too seriously. We wanted to stay as human as possible.

Our final hoorah as the Three Musketeers came at the end of training. We were finished with all the physical and mental tests, and every obstacle had been met and conquered. The final event on the schedule before graduation was a motivation run through the streets of Parris Island. McDonald, Gravett, and I worked through the night, preparing our final sendoff to the instructors who had kept us entertained and miserable for three long months.

We wrote a series of cadence songs just for them and would unveil them during the motivation run. Cadence is part of Marine Corps history and serves as a motivational tool that keeps you going during those lengthy runs. You've heard them before: marines clapping their hands, wearing the same shirts, and repeating whatever the cadence caller says. On this day, the cadence would be a little different.

We decided I would be the one to call the cadence. Gravett and McDonald didn't have the rhythm or memory for it. Looking back today, I think they realized whoever called the cadence would get a pretty big ass chewing, so now I know why I was picked. We tried to deliver a good-natured dig on each of the instructors, and the class of eighty soon-to-be DIs loved them. I'm not sure the instructors had the same reaction, but they knew we were as good as graduated, so they were good sports and didn't give us too much trouble.

> *First Sergeant, First Sergeant, don't be blue,*
> *A puppet on the Muppets has a gold tooth too . . .*

> *Gunnery Sergeant, Gunnery Sergeant, we know it's true,*
> *If we wore tight shirts we'd have big guns too . . .*

Graduation was bittersweet. School was over, and we all knew that what we had gone through was easy compared to what we were getting ready to face. Now we would actually have to make real marines. We would have to motivate, teach, train, inspire, and sometimes serve as the first and only dominant male figure in their lives. This would be the second hardest challenge I would face in my life, 110 hours and seven days a week and sleeping in camp every third night. Although I didn't know it at the time, this experience was exactly what I needed to prepare me for the most difficult challenge of my life: the job of being a single dad.

Most people think of drill instructors as unfeeling, unemotional, ugly bastards who yell all day long. While that's true (especially the ugly part), there's so much more to it than that. Our job is to strip recruits of their individuality and put them back together as a team. To some this seems inhuman, and I've heard it referred to as brainwashing. But it's not. For what we need to accomplish, it's critical. These young men have to learn to count on each other and use each other's strengths to accomplish their overall mission. You don't win wars alone, and you don't stay alive without your fellow marines. We need them to understand that, and the only way to get these young men to see it was to force them to experience complete exposure to and reliance upon each other.

The Famous Yellow Footprints

There isn't a marine on earth who forgets the day he or she arrived at Parris Island and stood at attention on the famous yellow footprints painted on the street. I've spent a lot of time with older marines through my charity work, and even eighty-year-old former marines reminisce about the day they arrived at boot camp. It's a moment that hits you like a brick, and you say to yourself, "What have I done, and how can I get out of this?"

There are a few behind-the-scenes activities that are not so well-known. For example, all recruits come in on a bus at around 2:00 a.m. Bringing the recruits in the wee hours of the evening keeps them discombobulated and unaware of their surroundings. It's hard to escape the island if you don't know where the exit is. There have been many attempts by recruits to escape, but it's dangerous to try. Parris Island is surrounded by swamps full of alligators and deep mud that can pull you under. It's not a prison, but we don't want recruits trying to negotiate swamps in the middle of the night. I had one recruit try to escape, a real Einstein who needed to plan his escape a whole lot better. In the middle of the night, he climbed into a Dumpster, figuring he would hitch a ride on an outgoing trash truck. He must have lost his nerve when he realized that the trip from the Dumpster to the truck was a pretty big fall. He screamed loud enough for the driver to hear, and disaster was averted. We dropped him, and he ended up going home anyway.

There are four stages to boot camp: receiving, phase 1, phase 2, and phase 3. Once recruits arrive, they are in receiving, the in-processing step that puts them through a series of paperwork drills, clothing issue, screaming, shots, medical screening, the famous first haircut, basic drills, and massive sleep deprivation. The first forty-eight hours are meant to keep them very uncomfortable. It's the beginning of the process of tearing them down and stripping away everything they know. They have no idea where they are going next, when they will sleep, when they will eat, and when some nasty thug in a Smokey the Bear hat will come and rip them apart. They make no decisions on their own, and even the simplest human privileges are removed. Going to the bathroom when you feel the urge and without permission will be something recruits learn to appreciate.

It's interesting to watch human behavior while recruits are going through all the stages of boot camp. I don't know if many of my fellow DIs took the time to observe this phenomenon as it unfolded, but I certainly did. Human beings always want to know what's going on, especially when it involves them. It's a basic principle for leaders in any industry, including financial advisors: communicate as much and as clearly as possible.

It's the most important leadership principle in the military or most jobs for that matter. There's a connection you need to make about communication that I definitely noticed during this time. When we didn't communicate to the recruits what was happening to them, they worked hard to try and figure it out using all their senses. You can't contain human behavior; it will break through any barrier you try to put up. And the outcome is usually counterproductive.

Think about it from a client's perspective. You control his or her financial future, you are in charge, and the client believes in you. Why, when everything fell apart in 2008, did so many advisors hide from their clients? Why weren't they proactively calling clients to instill confidence, show strength, compassion, and leadership?

Why is communication so vital? If you don't communicate, human nature takes over, and people start drawing their own conclusions. What happens then is that people start believing their own conclusions or they believe the person who seems to provide the most logical conclusion.

In 2007 and 2008, clients began to listen to reports on TV that the sky was falling, and they would be broke by end of day. Why wouldn't they believe the reports since there was no communication from their trusted advisor to offset the onslaught of negative media.

From the marine point of view, we denied the recruits any data or information. But, as humans, they tried to figure things out using their senses of smell, hearing, and sight. We marched them everywhere, but if you looked closely, you could see them imperceptibly moving their eyes, trying to analyze and collect data. They used their noses to try to figure out if they were near the chow hall when it was too dark to determine through sight.

It's where I learned that, as humans, we need data. We crave data to help us analyze our current situation, and we try to make educated guesses about what may happen next. The first time I marched my recruits to the chow hall, I could see their eyes taking pictures, entering the data into their brains/databases. (In the next chapter, I will talk about how to take the data that clients give you with every interaction and turn it into more meaningful contact.)

The second time I marched them, I used the same route and observed a change in their body language because they knew we were going to the chow hall. If you understand this behavior, you can use it to your advantage. I would march my recruits near the chow hall just to keep them guessing and end up taking an unexpected turn to another destination. It seems cruel, but it was part of the process to further reinforce that they were not in control.

Why is this important to an advisor, manager, or leader? Whether you like it or not, people will try to figure out what is going on. They will do it through data that is available to them. I've observed this on many occasions and in very different circumstances. Whether it was the Marine Corps or Merrill Lynch, lack of communication always led to a lack of productivity, a poor work environment and, ultimately, unhappy clients.

During the market crash in 2008 and the subsequent purchase of Merrill Lynch by Bank of America, there was a complete breakdown in communication. Our leaders made many calls and conducted numerous conferences only to say they had nothing to report. This caused a frenzy of speculation that destroyed morale.

When people are worried about their livelihood and families, what do you think is going to happen if you don't provide them with comfort and information? Some leaders say they have nothing to report. I say give the people the plan, tell them what you're thinking, tell them what you can, and recognize that they're searching for answers. It would later be discovered how much our leaders did know about what was happening to Merrill. The leadership failed, and it's what brought our mighty bull to its knees. Shame on them for taking their eye off the ball. If they remembered the golden rule, that the client's interest must come first, we may not have been in the situation in the first place.

When humans search for information, it's not always for the obvious things. It can be a simple gesture that is out of the norm or a change in a senior manager's routine that can cause speculation to fly through your company. I remember when the head of marketing at Merrill Lynch scheduled a conference call during the most turbulent months. There were people tracking her flights, calls, and trips to New York and Boston. Every piece of data caused more speculation.

For leaders, it's important to understand that you can't stop people from communicating, collecting data, and thinking, so you might as well communicate everything you have. Speculation and rumors are unproductive and unnecessary. If you are planning layoffs, let people know. The corporate world drives me crazy when they hide layoffs. Don't they know their employees have already heard rumors, and those rumors have kept everyone unproductive and unmotivated for weeks and months?

The military tells its troops that they are going into battle and prepare for it. They don't hide it; they communicate and give their people the information they must have to help them prepare for every eventuality.

For recruits, the objective is to keep them guessing and make sure they know they aren't in control. We also understand that human nature cannot be stopped, and they will continue to look for data and trends.

As a platoon leader, I trained myself to sleep with the light on in the barracks every third night. I would set my watch alarm to buzz every two hours so I could get up, get completely dressed, and summon the recruit standing watch. I did this when I realized the recruits were tracking my sleep patterns and would wait until I went to sleep before getting up to write letters. Sleeping with the light on and coming out every two hours completely dressed actually made them think I never slept so they couldn't track my sleep patterns.

We also noticed the recruits' collective mood changed when certain instructors were scheduled to sleep in the barracks. We realized that a certain instructor was being overly nice to the recruits and allowing extra time for letters and showers. So to keep them guessing, we changed our patterns and switched sleeping nights every week or two. And we gave Mr. Nice Instructor a good ass chewing for being a big brother to the recruits and not doing his job.

The lesson is that throughout the three months recruits are on the island, they continue to collect data, draw conclusions, and work to figure out what's coming next. Just remember that your clients are doing the same thing. You can hide in your office and turn off the phone, but that doesn't solve the problem. If you don't know what's going on, share that with your clients, but give them your plan. And if you don't have one, *get one.*

Your job is extremely important; you are the financial leader who is basically in charge of your clients' financial future and freedom. This is a major responsibility and a huge burden you've chosen to take on. Lead your clients, inspire them, show them you are confident and in control, and communicate with them constantly. If you don't, they'll find the data on their own, and you may no longer be the one they'll turn to. That's human nature.

Notes

Notes

Notes

Notes

Notes

CHAPTER 4

EXCEEDING EXPECTATIONS

If you take nothing else from this book, remember this chapter because it's the *most* important thing I teach financial advisors. The model I lay out can actually be applied to any business or any career; it's the key to success and the foundation for a lifelong relationship with your clients.

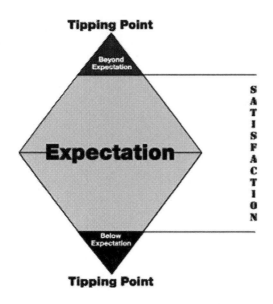

If you get this, you can succeed in *anything*!

I can pinpoint the exact moment in my life when I learned that the little details make a big difference. I was about twelve years old and working for my stepdad in the family business, which was racing horses. Standard-bred horses, to be specific, which are the one used in harness racing (the races with the little cart behind the horse).

It was a dirty business in every sense of the word. My job was to muck (clean) the horse stalls. It was good money for a young kid, and it's where I developed my work ethic. I learned the powerful lesson that you should do a job right the first time. My mother, who also worked as a groom for my stepdad, inspected the stalls with an eagle eye and showed absolutely no compassion for a weary kid who just wanted to get paid and play video games. I used to get so mad when she made me clean the stalls over and over again. She would point and say, "Did you see that or that or that . . ." It took time, but I finally realized that doing it right the first time was much quicker and less frustrating than doing it over.

Many hours were spent in those stalls, and I had a lot of time to think. What did I want to do with my life? Who did I want to be when I grew up? I always knew I wouldn't go into the family business even though I loved it. The problem was that it was so unpredictable, moneywise. The amount of food that filled our cabinets was directly related to whether or not a horse won a race, and that uncertainty is what turned me from the business. To this day, I can relive the hours I spent watching races and praying for this or that horse to win so we could have a full cupboard and a working phone.

My stepdad wasn't flashy, just a very hard worker and extremely smart when it came to training horses. I would often see other trainers come to him for advice about their horses. He was like the horse whisperer and had an uncommon bond with these majestic creatures. He was highly respected and was ranked as one of the top ten trainers at the racetrack in our hometown.

I often sat in the racetrack cafeteria with a racing program and a bacon-and-egg sandwich and marveled that my stepdad was listed in the program as one of the top trainers. But even with that respect, his barn never grew bigger than ten horses even during his best years. A good producing barn would have twenty to thirty horses.

How could this be? I asked myself over and over. You would think that the best trainer, the person who knew the most about horses would be the one who is most successful. Right? Not even close.

So who were the successful trainers?
They were the ones with the flashy trucks with their names painted almost boastfully on the doors. They were the ones with the massive stables that were kept meticulously clean. They were the ones whose horses had personalized bridles with the horses' names etched on them, and each stall had a gold plaque with each horse's name on it. To the right of each stall, uniformly placed like soldiers in a row, were handsome equipment trunks with the stable logo on the front and the horse's name on the top. Every groom and assistant trainer had shirts and jackets with the name of their stable embroidered. Every trainer had a rich-looking office where he entertained owners who could become clients.

I used to ask my stepdad why we didn't have matching trunks, jackets, and shirts, things that would make us look like we were as good as those other stables. My stepfather would grunt and mutter, "It's all about what you know and how you train the horses that matters." He didn't believe in flashy marketing; he just didn't see the value. And in a logical world, he would have been right. In that world, people would look for the trainer with the most knowledge, not the best marketing. Unfortunately, however, this is not a logical world, and my stepfather's stubbornness was his biggest mistake. Our stable would never be as successful as it should have been.

If you chart my stepfather's business on the diagram and look at what satisfaction is and where the tipping points were, then you start to understand how this works.

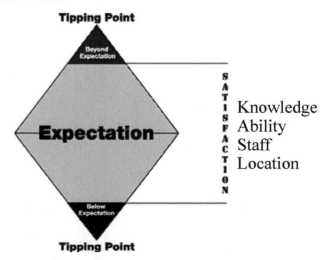

My stepfather prided himself on doing the things that were expected, things that provided satisfaction. But satisfaction doesn't get a customer walking away feeling euphoric. And you can apply that to other "customers" such as your spouse, your children, and your life. How are you constantly raising the bar and excelling beyond *their* expectations? That's the question I want you to ask yourself, and then draw the diagram. If you just apply the satisfaction meter and identify what the expectations are, you have a better shot at exceeding those expectations—and that's where you find the tipping points.

Tipping points are things that occur when (a) you've gone *beyond* what a customer expects and that customer's perception changes in a positive direction or (b) you've gone *below* what is expected of you and the perception changes the other way. In other words, you start to lose business. The problem is, you don't know where people's tipping point is. You only know how to constantly deliver things that could trigger the tip.

When I first started traveling for Merrill Lynch, the Ritz Carlton was Merrill Lynch's hotel of choice. Now I didn't have much experience with the Ritz Carlton chain, but I certainly knew its legendary reputation for ultimate client service. My first interaction with a Ritz was in the Detroit area. My expectations were through the roof, and I wondered how they would exceed expectations. Based on their brand, they would really need to work hard to hit the tipping point with me. Unfortunately, they underdelivered in three areas: their rooms were old and tired (at least mine was), their technology was surprisingly dated, and their fitness equipment was simply unacceptable. For me, they tipped below expectations, and I never went to another Ritz Carlton.

Look, I was a poor kid from the sticks, and they should have been able to knock my socks off with a pillow mint. Instead, they found a way to tip me to the negative. For you and your business to thrive, you must understand that no one knows where the tipping points are. It could be as simple as a client leaving because of one missed phone call, or fifteen missed phone calls. What we do know for sure is that if you play near the *below expectation* area, you are putting yourself in a place where you risk a negative tipping point. If you play in the *expectation* space, you will achieve satisfaction, but in some relationships, that might not be enough to gain loyalty and trust. And finally, if you play in the *above expectation* area, it's likely you will find a tipping point to the positive and achieve the loyalty and trust that is so critical to your success as a financial advisor.

Let's go back to the horses. Where were the tipping points, both good and bad? My stepfather's knowledge of the business was definitely extraordinary, but he would not find a tipping point with his knowledge. In this case, people needed their trainers to appear credible, and credibility can be found in some very strange places. Some of the trainers with the flashy cars and mansion-like stables were idiots, but it didn't matter. They *looked* the part, and that is what many customers wanted. They wanted to walk in and feel that their investment was safe. They wanted to bring family members to see their horse and feel like a VIP. It didn't matter that the trainer mistreated the horse or overcharged the owner. All that mattered was that the customers' needs were met.

In his stubbornness to keep to his values as one of the best trainers in the business, my stepfather missed the voice of the customer. People who are buying a horse want to be treated like royalty. They want the trappings of success, illusory or not. The common man with a regular job doesn't wake up one day and decide he wants to own a racehorse. Horse buyers are often people who have money or just came into money. They want the finer things in life, and believe me, it's not just the racehorse they want. It's the glitz and glamour that goes with it.

Remember that it's not always what we think is important—or should be important—to our clients that matter. It's what *they* think that's important. This concept is often difficult for financial advisors to grasp because they tend to be wrapped up in the investing, the market, the financial products, and the actual job of managing clients' money. FAs assume that their knowledge of the market will be the tipping point for their less-than-knowledgeable clients. Guess what? It's *not*!

Don't get me wrong. I'm not saying investments, performance, operations, and service aren't important. They're the foundation, but they're also what's *expected*. Your clients and prospects expect you to know and completely understand the market. You're a financial advisor, for goodness' sakes! Of course, you know about the market. That is satisfaction, and *satisfaction is the cost of doing business*. You won't find the tipping point in your knowledge of the market. You'll find that tipping points usually have nothing to do with investments.

One night, my wife and I were watching a wonderful show on MSNBC called *The Building of the Brand McDonald's*. It was a detailed study of how the company started and why it became one of the largest franchises in the world. MSNBC went to the most successful McDonald's in the world—located on I-95 in Connecticut—to interview the owner and business manager to gain an understanding of how and why their franchise was so successful.

The news team asked the business manager what he thought was the key to the success of this McDonald's. I immediately hit pause on the TiVo and told my wife that I could guess the answer. But I didn't follow my own diagram for expectations, and I responded as most people would. I guessed it was the french fries. I believed that McDonald's made the fries every thirty seconds to ensure that everyone enjoyed the exact same taste experience. I had been disappointed from time to time at various McDonald's when I received dark yellow, limp, and tepid fries. I truly think they are the foundation for the menu, the rock upon which the franchise stands.

But what I missed is that while great fries might be the foundation, they are also part of our expectation and satisfaction. We expect the fries to be perfect when we walk in the door, and we're not blown away merely because we're satisfied. (Same with our jobs, by the way.)

I was wrong, but I insisted on trying to pinpoint the key success factor—even though my wife wanted me to just hit play on the TiVo. I had the remote, so I won. Anyway, my next guess was customer service. Had to be, I thought, because McDonald's pays a lot of attention to customer service and ensures that every patron receives a greeting, a smile, and a very friendly atmosphere. But, once again, I was playing in the space of expectation. It's possible to go beyond expectations in this area, but this particular McDonald's simply met already high expectations.

My last guess was speed. I figured they had a huge timing device of some sort and consistently worked to get the food to each customer faster and faster. The funny thing is, when you look at expectations for McDonald's, you can start with the name of the industry: fast food. If fast service isn't expected in an industry called fast food, then I don't know what is. No, speed is to be expected and is not the reason for their success.

Are you ready for the answer? My wife sure was as she ripped the remote from my hands and hit play on the TiVo.

It was the bathrooms!

Are you kidding me? The bathrooms? That's what the world's most successful McDonald's said. They believe that if their bathrooms are clean, the customer will come back, and if they're not clean, customers won't return. And that's why they clean their bathrooms every fifteen minutes.

It's hard to argue with the most successful McDonald's anywhere on the planet, but I tried anyway. I took my expectation/satisfaction diagram and ripped apart their claim. Let's work through it: What's your expectation for bathroom cleanliness in a fast food establishment? What's been your overall experience? How clean are the bathrooms?

Over time, your expectation for bathroom cleanliness in fast-food restaurants has probably diminished, probably dramatically. This particular McDonald's realized they had found an area where they could go well beyond expectations—just by cleaning its restrooms. What they are driving toward is the customer's feeling of surprise, even pleasure, when walking into a sparkling clean bathroom. While some people may not notice how clean the bathrooms are, many others will. Many will get it on a subliminal level, where a brain impulse registers that this is much better than I expected.

Let's consider where/how you can exceed expectations in your business.

How important is the marketing?
Think about how you might interview a cleaning company for your home. How would you feel about a person who comes to your house in frayed jeans, drives a Toyota Corolla, and his only marketing material is a light blue flyer that looks like it was xeroxed too many times? The

next interviewee walks in with a crisp bright yellow polo shirt with a company logo prominently, but tastefully, displayed on the shirt. He hands you a splashy trifold four-color brochure that includes a photo of a fleet of PT Cruisers—each with the company logo professionally screened on its doors—which matches the one in the driveway. The guy in the picture, the one standing in front of the fleet of cars, happens to be the same person who's standing in front of you, talking about his cleaning business.

With both prices comparable, with which of the two cleaning companies would you be more likely to do business?

In most cases, you would go with the fleet of cars, the professionally crafted brochure, and the nice polo shirt. Does it matter that the fleet of cars are photoshopped and don't really exist? Does it matter that the brochure was composed on a Mac and printed at home on glossy paper picked up at Staples? Perhaps it would if you had that background info, but most people simply look at the line of cars, the flashy brochure and shirt, and find credibility and comfort. To keep the relationship, of course, the cleaning company will need to cover expectations by ensuring your house is cleaned properly and to go beyond expectations with unexpected flourishes, even ones as simple as maybe "cornering" toilet paper as they do in fine hotels.

American Maid

A few years ago, a friend asked if I could help him expand his maid-service business. He wasn't sure where or how to start, and he needed some marketing ideas. His business was small and wasn't growing at the pace he had envisioned. While my friend was a good businessperson, he was not a great marketer. He prided himself on how well his friendly and efficient staff cleaned homes, and he assumed that would be enough to have referrals pour in. That's not what happened.

The first thing I did was ask him to read a book called the *Tipping Point* by Malcolm Gladwell. (You'll see more about this book in the Prospecting chapter.) The book drives home my point that "little things" will end up changing your business. I knew the changes I was going to suggest would seem minor and, perhaps insignificant, to a brilliant young man who was caught up in the world of covering satisfaction.

My friend groaned and said, "Are you seriously asking me to read a book? Can't you just design a new brochure and ad for me? That should be good enough." I explained that he needed to understand the foundation so he could completely understand what I was about to do with his business. He grudgingly went off to read the book, and I sat down to chart expectations for a cleaning company.

I started with my diagram: what is satisfaction for a maid-service business? My friend was doing exactly what I expected and what his customers expected: arrive when scheduled, clean the house, and be courteous. I thought for days about how he could exceed expectations and get to loyalty and trust as a way to generate much-needed referrals. I recommended four changes that created a flood of referrals and expanded his business dramatically:

Chocolate Coins

We had chocolate coins made with his logo imprinted on the front and back. I suggested he do a turn-down service in every bedroom, with one of his coins on a pillow, just as the Ritz Carlton maid service would. While my friend thought that was a silly idea, he trusted me enough to try it, and it turned out to be even more successful than I imagined possible. *What happened?* His customers' children started asking when the cleaners were coming. Kids paying attention to how the house is cleaned? And endorsing us? How perfect was that? My friend couldn't believe the impact of "silly" chocolate coins, but the proof couldn't be denied.

Toilet Paper

I asked my friend to stock all his cleaning vehicles with rolls and rolls of toilet paper. And I suggested he place a brand-new roll of toilet paper in every bathroom, no matter how much was left on the existing roll. I also asked him to take it one step further and, over time, determine if the client used a particular type of toilet paper and replace it with that specific brand. We ordered small oval gold stickers with his company's initials on them. Then he folded the corners and put the gold tabs on, just as the Ritz would. *What do you think the feedback was?* People loved it because it was different, unexpected, and gave the impression of white-glove service that makes you feel special.

What a wonderful feeling to know that someone is taking the time to attend to your needs. Think about your business. What do you do every day to make your clients feel special, to make them feel as if they are the only ones you are thinking about? If you can't answer that question, keep reading! By the end of this chapter, you'll have a clear understanding of how to set a path to achieve what will set you apart from every other financial advisor.

The Tent Card
We had a small tent card made that read "Complimentary Cleaning from American Maid." The reason? I suggested that at each home, a staff member goes into the refrigerator or cupboards or linen closet or other area from time to time. Take everything out, clean it, and put it back. Then leave the tent card displayed so the customer could realize their cleaning service went way beyond expectation. The staff never said a word; the card did all the talking. And the feedback was off the charts.

The Follow-Up Call
The last change was something I couldn't believe wasn't already being done. I thought it was standard and expected but soon realized it's rarely done.

When dealing with many (most?) service companies, our expectations are lower than they should be. Why do we allow this? Why don't we demand better service? How surprised would you be if your lawnmower service called after every cutting, just to check and be sure everything was good to go and to see if you needed additional services? That should be something all service companies do. And that's exactly what I wanted added to my friend's service.

I insisted that the follow-up call had to be made by *him*, not by an administrative or customer relations person. Every night, he would make courtesy calls to each of that day's customers to ensure they were satisfied with their cleaning. Because he was the boss, he had the power to remedy *any* problems he discovered during his courtesy calls. If something hadn't been done properly, he could make sure it was resolved the very next morning. This is the step that ensured the three previous steps weren't washed away by a silent complaint that went unanswered.

We added splashy marketing and matching polo shirts for everyone on my friend's staff. Did it all work? *Yes*! He achieved loyalty and trust because he covered expectations when cleaning customers' homes, and he went *beyond* expectations in other areas. The word of mouth we generated was unbelievable, and his business increased over the next year by 50 percent.

Incidentally, even with all the "gimmicks" and "feel good" services, without good quality control, the best marketing can't cover up shoddy work. Unless you cover the basic expectation—in this case, a well-cleaned home—you will not have the opportunity to achieve the tipping points that can take you beyond expectation.

There's an age-old question of whether or not marketing works. The analytical people, the number crunchers, want facts and figures that demonstrate how marketing is contributing to the bottom line. The problem with that is, you can't always measure it. How do you affix a number to someone who reads your ad and makes a mental note about you and your advisory service? Especially when his financial advisor dies months later, but he remembers you from your ad, gives you a call and, ultimately, his business?

Unless you do significant research to determine how every prospect and client heard about you, you can't capture the power of marketing, branding, and awareness. To the numbers guys, those hunched-over creatures of the calculator, my message is *chill out*! Marketing is about setting the tone, building the brand, tilling the soil. It all has a cumulative impact.

Sunshine Decks

Several years ago, I was introduced to my sister's boyfriend who built decks for a living. We talked for hours about how he could increase his business through simple marketing and branding. He had just started a partnership with a friend, and they were doing "okay," but with a little help, they could double their business.

The partner was a typical construction guy: no sense of customer service, no marketing or branding to speak of. I spent a ton of time giving both of them ideas on growing the business, but the reluctant partner simply couldn't see the value in investing in marketing and branding. He couldn't see the power of a yellow trailer with a *big* Sunshine Decks logo on all four sides, a glossy brochure, the works. So I decided to do an experiment that would shake the foundation of my wonderful marriage. I would keep my job at Merrill Lynch but open a Sunshine Decks company in my hometown to show how powerful marketing and branding can be.

Before I continue, you should understand that I'm not a handyman (understatement!). In fact, I can't even hang a picture straight. When my wife told me to just find a stud, I went next door and brought back the neighbors' strapping nineteen-year-old son and told him to hang the damned picture. I don't understand how electricians run cables through walls without knocking down the entire wall. I have no idea how to cut a tile or why it needs water, and guess what, I don't want to know. It's not my thing.

I'm a marketing guy who specializes in sales, branding, and public speaking. I don't have any interest in remodeling. You need this background to understand what happened when I told my wife I was about to open a deck business and invest $10,000 as a *test*. She had a serious problem with it. She asked me if I knew what a footer was (not sure how she knew this herself, but I think she had some coaching). Of course, I had no idea. She glared at me and said, "It's the foundation of a deck, you moron. How do you expect to sell something if you don't even know how it's built?"

I told her I'd do a little research, but that it didn't really matter. My test was to see how powerful marketing and branding could be. If I looked credible, had all the proper marketing and logos in place, could I sell a deck? I was sure I could because I wouldn't have invested the money.

I started with the basics and developed a logo, good-looking T-shirts, company checks, invoices, business cards, even acquired computer software that could design a deck.

My next move was a call to my friends at Donnelley InfoUSA to rent a list of ten thousand names from one zip code, all of which had an approximate net worth of $800,000. (There's more on how to pull a list in the direct mail portion of this book.) Then I created a large, glossy postcard mailing and used royalty-free photos (in other words, virtually no cost) of completed decks to set the stage. My offer to recipients of the mailing was for a free gas grill—perfect for a new deck—if a purchase was made in the month of July.

I received ten calls, got appointments to go to seven of them, and sold one deck for $35,000. I went home with a deposit of $5,000. (Not bad for a mailing that cost around $2,000!) So how did I do it since I knew nothing about building decks? It was *all* marketing and relationship building. And just to put your mind at ease, I found a great deck builder who built the deck to expectation. I didn't make any money, but then again, I didn't lose any money either. But I was thrilled with the results from my experiment. And my wife is still talking to me.

The Expectation Model for FAs

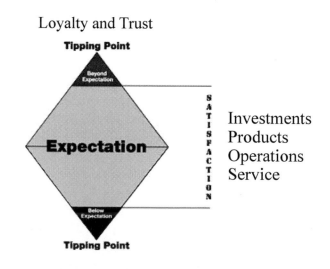

Now that you "get" expectation and understand why it's important to exceed expectation, let's get specific about expectations for financial advisors and how you reach loyalty and trust.

You've heard it over and over again from speakers, sales managers, top execs, and your fellow FAs: to be successful, you must build loyalty and trust. In the world of financial advisors, there are two roads that can get you to loyalty and trust, and we're going to look at each one.

The first is extremely effective. In fact, nothing will get you to the top of the pyramid faster and nothing will build loyalty and trust more quickly than *performance*. Good performance and consistent results will have your clients loving you. Great performance will skyrocket you to the top of the pyramid and the field.

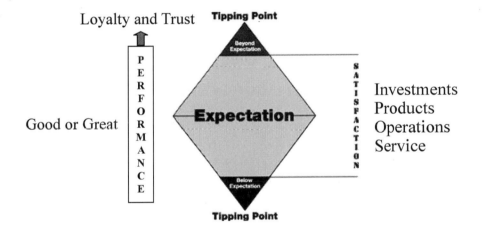

The problem with this method is that you don't control it, and you can't sustain it. Many of the advisors I worked with over the last few years built their entire client relationships on performance. But when the markets went south, what were they left with? Nothing. Once performance was gone, there was no reason for a client to stay. It's not a sound, long-term approach to getting to the top of the pyramid.

The second road to loyalty and trust is in the *relationship*. If you can build a deep relationship with your clients, if you can truly understand and articulate their needs, hopes, and dreams, if you can grasp what they feel and want for their children, grandchildren, and legacy, this is what really bonds clients to their financial advisor.

Loyalty and Trust

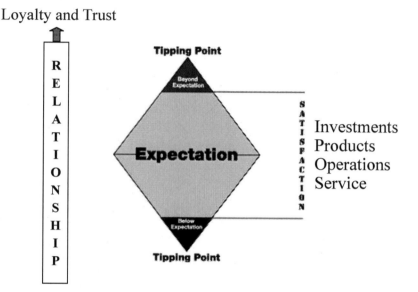

Well, that's easy to say. Go forth and build a relationship. Over the years, I've seen so-called experts pump up financial advisors with that advice. But that's also where the experts fail because they can't offer the actionable steps that develop the kind of relationship that builds long-term loyalty and trust.

You have success at hand. When your finished reading this segment and book, you will know how to go deeper with your clients and be certain you're in tune with whatever is going on in their lives and have a greater understanding of their specific needs.

The silver bullet is *data*, the information you gather on your clients and prospects that helps you make meaningful contact with them. It seems so easy, but I'm no longer amazed at how many FAs don't know how to use their data effectively—if they use it (or even have it) at all.

Capturing and Mining Your Data

Data is the key to forming a closer/stronger bond with clients. A few years ago, I saw a study where clients of a full service brokerage firm were asked what was most important to them about their financial advisor. Over 70 percent responded that the relationship was most important. And that got me thinking. If the relationship is the most important thing, how would an FA go about kicking that up a notch, going deeper with a client?

It's all in the data. The data drives everything. It controls how much you know about your clients, and it also helps you find common bonds with them. When you change your business and start capturing data at every opportunity, it will become habit-forming. This will *force* you to *listen* to your clients and prospects, and get them talking. I hope you're not one of those advisors who think they're paid to talk and rarely listen because **listening generates valuable data.**

I once met with an extremely successful Midwest advisor who was on the *Barron's* Top 100 list, year after year. He told me about the first meeting he went on many years ago with his mentor and trainer, a gentleman who had been in the business for over thirty years. When the FA finished the meeting, he was excited that it went so well . . . until he realized his mentor was glaring at him. He asked what was wrong, and the wise older man replied, "Don't you ever shut up? These people wanted to tell you about their hopes and dreams. They wanted to talk about what's going on in their lives. They don't want to hear you talk. The more you let them talk, the more you will find out about them, so next time, take my advice and *shut up*." That was an eye-opener for the FA, a real-life lesson, and he's carried it with him throughout his very successful career.

The Test

Since many advisors think they already do a good job at capturing and mining data, I'm going to take you through a little test to help you assess how well you capture data and how well you mine it. Here is the scenario:

I'm your client, and I have approximately $3 million—all my assets—in my account. I'm a good client. I've been with you for about six years, and we get along great. You know my wife, and we exchange holiday cards every year. We talk every couple of months, but I'm about ten years away from retirement, so I'm diversified and don't watch the balance go up and down. On one of your recent calls, you asked me what was going on, and I excitedly replied that I had forgotten to tell you our oldest daughter, Brittany, was accepted to West Virginia University. Andy (my wife) and I are upset and happy at the same time. We were hoping she would stay in New Jersey. Andy is worried because she will be six hours away and at one of the biggest party schools in the country. Brittany, on the other hand, is EXCITED because she'll be six hours away and at one of the biggest party schools in the country. I'll let you know how I feel in September after she leaves for college. Talk to you in a couple months, goodbye . . .

My question is simple. After you hung up the phone with the client, what would you do with the information the client gave you? Would you put the seemingly insignificant nugget or two of data into a system?

Before you answer that question, let me say that I don't care how you save the data, I don't care which system you use, be it Salesforce, ACT, GoldMine, Excel spreadsheet, or yellow sticky notes. All I'm concerned with is that you save the data somewhere other than in your head, which seems to be the preferred method for many, many FAs. Unless you have a photographic memory like the Dustin Hoffman character in *Rain Man*, the data will leave your brain at some point. Period.

Everyone must put this kind of data into a system. I worked with a *huge* producer on the West Coast who writes all the information he gathers on client folders. When he fills up a folder, he adds a new one. Whatever works, I guess. But my issue with that advisor is that you can't do a search on terms with folders, and that makes it a little more labor-intensive to mine the data than it should be.

I've run this same scenario with over three thousand financial advisors in my travels across the country, and here are the numbers:

- *Twenty percent* are sure that when presented with that scenario above, they will store the data in their system. I'm constantly shocked by that low number.
- Eighty percent say they don't capture the data at all.

The next question only applies to the 20 percent who actually save the data. I ask if they put a reminder in their calendar to do some kind of follow-up in the August/September time frame to see how the family is doing. (Most freshmen leave for college in August—a significant event in your clients' lives, don't you think?)

The numbers drop significantly on this question. Only *5 percent* of the 20 percent say they will schedule a follow-up call with the client. That tells me that while 20 percent of the advisors actually capture the data, only 5 percent of them are actually mining it. Why bother to capture data if you aren't going to use it? If you're not going to use it to go deeper with your client which is *exactly* what clients want—why waste your time?

Where do you fit in so far? Are you capturing the data? Are you mining it?

For the last question, and an even more dramatic drop in numbers, did you identify three follow-up calls with three separate people in that scenario? Don't feel bad if you couldn't identify three people because fewer than *one-half of one percent* of FAs actually see and schedule three separate contacts with three separate people. Who were they? Let's break it down:

The Client

This is the easy one. You reach out to the client and see how they are doing. Does the child need an account or debit card at school? Yes, this is Relationship Building 101?—but only five percent of advisors actually do it.

The Spouse

On Main Street USA in the 1950s, who made the financial decisions in the house? The husband or the wife? It was almost always the husband; rarely did the wife even have a say in how the finances were managed. My, how things have changed in the sixty years since the man was in complete control of everything except the cooking, as this 2008 study from the Pew Research Center demonstrates:

Who makes the decisions at home?

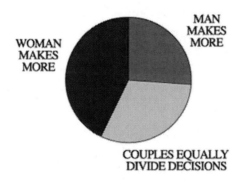

Results based on responses to questions on choosing shared weekend activities, buying things in the home, deciding what to watch on television and managing houshold finances.

Now, whether you believe the study or not, you must agree that women today have a seat at the table and, in many cases, are at the head of the table. The problem is when advisors refuse to change their contact strategy and still operate as if the male client is the only one with whom it's necessary to build a relationship. Do *not* forget the spouse because he or she has a say when it comes to hiring or firing *you*! In this scenario, almost all advisors miss the follow-up contact with the spouse, a prime opportunity to build a deeper bond. The American household is no longer the Cleavers or Ozzie and Harriet. The world has changed, and it's time to revamp your contact strategy!

The Child

Virtually every advisor misses the contact with Brittany who, of course, represents the next generation. Firms are losing clients rapidly as the next generation is redefining how they will retire, when they will retire, and who will manage their investments. I've had hundreds of conversations with FAs who tell me their dilemma is that their clients are dying and they need help with a strategy to build a deeper relationship with the next generation of clients. The problem is they're too late.

People aren't stupid. They know why you are reaching out to them. Their parents are ninety and they are fifty-five to sixty, and the question is, "Where have you been for the last twenty years?" Are you up-to-date with the next generation? Did you reach out when they started college? Or when they got their first job? First checking account? First mortgage? Had their first child? If the answer is no, you have absolutely no relationship with the next generation and their response to you is, "Who are you, and why should I automatically give you my business?"

Just because you manage their parents' finances doesn't give you a free pass to the kids. In the scenario I laid out, I gave thousands of advisors the opportunity for contact, and almost all of them missed it. Yet all of them cry about losing the next generation. Well, stop crying and start doing something about it. Start saving data: kids' names, birthdates, interests, everything. In this scenario, most FAs light up and say, "Yes, I could have sent her some investment material." And I respond that, yeah, that's exactly what Brittany wants on her way to college—investment brochures. Speak the language of the next generation, know the customer, do a little research on West Virginia University, and find the popular café that all kids go to. Get a gift certificate to that café and send a card with the following note:

Brittany,

You are about to embark on the greatest four years of your life—enjoy them. I set up a debit card for you and gave it to your mother. If you have any problem, call me or your parents and we'll get it fixed ASAP. You may not know about the café listed on the enclosed gift certificate, but you will when you get to WVU, so have your first dinner on me. Good luck!

Sincerely,
[Name of Financial Advisor]

Building a strong relationship with the next generation of your clients should be a top priority for you because it's where I've seen the majority of advisors lose assets. I spent some time with an advisor in the south who explained that the majority of the business he's losing is coming from clients who are passing away, and he's not getting the next generation. His best existing client is eighty-five, but the wife has taken over all financial responsibilities since the client had a stroke this year.

I asked the advisor if the family had an eightieth birthday party for his client. The advisor looked at me with a confused expression on his face. The reason I asked that question was because what I really wanted to know was whether or not he was invited to the birthday party. The answer, obviously, was no. And that's a problem. The FA's relationship was not deep enough to warrant an invitation.

Family parties and gatherings are the places where your clients' children will notice that your relationship is much more than advisor-client; it's friend-friend. If you're not operating with this mentality, the first place where the next generation will see you will be at their parents' funeral. When you're kneeling at the casket, it's a little too late. I know this is harsh, but you must face facts: the money is shifting to the next generation, and when that generation gets old, it will shift again and again and again. You can either start now or try to play catch-up later.

Saving and mining important data will change the way you do business and help you go deeper with your clients and prospects.

A financial advisor approached me after a presentation and told me he's been capturing and mining data for years. He's always amazed at how many advisors don't, and he's equally amazed at how well it continues to work for growing and cultivating his book. He started years ago with an Excel spreadsheet (I also use Excel for capturing data), listing first name, last name, address, phone number, and *notes*. The notes column is where the money was. He annotated every piece of data he could gather, no matter how insignificant he thought it was at the time.

He went on to tell me that the data was how he was able to identify that one of his clients was having a twenty-fifth wedding anniversary. He read through his notes on that client to see what could help him go a little deeper than a card and found what he was looking for. There was a note from a conversation where the client was telling him what an amazing weekend he had with his wife at a bed-and-breakfast about forty miles outside of town. The client said they had the time of their life there. That data helped the FA send the client a gift certificate and a Happy Anniversary card with the following inscription:

Bob and Mary,

I remember you went to this bed-and-breakfast five years ago and had a wonderful time. I thought you might like to go back. Have a wonderful twenty-fifth anniversary.

Sincerely,
[Name of Financial Advisor]

Bam! That's a contact! Is your data good enough to send a card to your clients? Do you even know the anniversary date of your clients? Do you send your clients birthday cards? You probably do, and I'll applaud you for it, but your birthday card sits in the mailbox with a slew of the other birthday cards from real estate agents, car salesmen, CPAs, attorneys, and anyone else they may have done business with over the past five years. Do you put yourself in the same category as the real estate agent or car salesman? If not, then why are you operating like them? Your relationship is deeper than that, you are more important than they are, so all I'm asking you to do is raise your game so you don't appear to be the same as them.

Hilton, I'm a Diamond Member. So What?

The concept of saving data is so basic you would think everyone is doing it, but that just isn't so. I've stayed in Hilton hotels for well over three hundred nights in countless number of cities and towns across the country. You would think they could tell you everything about me. What I like to drink, what I like to eat for dinner, how much I need a good fitness center, and numerous other details. You may be surprised to find they actually know *nothing*. They do not save data, and if a local Hilton actually saved something, it's not shared across the Hilton enterprise. Why? I don't know, but it drives me crazy to think about the golden opportunities they miss on hundreds of thousands of guests.

I take every chance I can to counsel local managers on the pyramid and how expectation is not what's going to keep me loyal to Hilton. Without the little extra-relationship things, what keeps me there? Nothing! If Marriott gives me a good offer, I'll leave in a heartbeat. As a Hilton Diamond member, you would expect that when I check into a hotel the greeting would be spectacular since the Hilton is like my second home—but it isn't. While the associate checking me in has the data right in front of her, the company has not built the culture to use the data. For about 95 percent of the time, the greeting is:

> *Mr. Clemenko, welcome to the Hilton, we have your Honors number on file and thank-you for your loyalty.*

Geez, if the Hilton is my second home, imagine getting that greeting in my first home.

> *Hi, honey, welcome to your home, food is in the refrigerator, and we thank you for earning the money.*

If the Hilton wanted to kick it up a notch, all they have to do is use the data that is right in front of their faces. I would think the greeting should go something like this:

> *Mr. Clemenko, welcome to our Hilton, thank-you for your loyalty, you are one of the family. Is there anything I can do to*

make your stay more special? The general manager left his card for you as we've been anticipating your arrival and said to call him anytime, day or night, if you have a problem. My name is —, you can also call me as I'll be here all evening.

I timed this, and it takes approximately twenty seconds to say. Plus, it costs *nothing*. It drives home that a Diamond member is different, and it's the kind of greeting that goes beyond my expectation. That's what builds loyalty and trust, and that's what will stop me from leaving for the Marriott when they offer a fire sale or extra points giveaway. I had a close friend tell me it's impossible to give the type of service I expect without the hotel having to pay higher salaries. I think that's a cop-out, actually simpleminded. It's about building a culture that cultivates relationships and puts a spotlight on the power of the little things to captivate customers.

I believe that in the life cycle of a relationship, there are thousands of opportunities to exceed a person's expectations. My question is whether or not you *see* the opportunity when it presents itself. And if you do see it, *do you seize it?* Capture and mine the data, and that will be the differentiator between you and your competition.

Embassy Suites, Dallas, Texas

I took this photo after I checked into my room at the Embassy Suites outside of Dallas, Texas. I had stayed there a few weeks before and had a nice conversation with the manager. He obviously understood the value of capturing data because, on my next visit, I was pleasantly surprised (in other words, my expectation was surpassed) with a beautiful food display and the inscription "Semper Fi" written in chocolate. Will I stay there the next time I'm in Dallas? You bet I will. The manager captured my data, saved it, and then used the data to go deeper with me. "Semper Fi," as you may know, is a term used by marines; in my conversation with the manager, I must have brought up that I was a former marine *Bam*! That's a contact! And a lifetime customer.

Creating a Lasting Impression

After meeting a prospect, what's the impression you leave? What do you mail as a follow-up to make sure that the prospect remembers you? If you don't do this sort of activity, it's time for you to start thinking about what I consider a crucial relationship-building tool. Many advisors don't send anything, not even a handwritten note to thank the prospect for his or her time. And if your mailing is a business card and a brochure, you're still missing the mark. That's what every run-of-the-mill advisor does, but it doesn't have the *wow* factor that serves as a differentiator.

The Follow-up Coin Was a Near-Magical Solution

When I started building relationships with Merrill Lynch managers in the field, I knew I would need something to send as a follow-up to my visits. What would leave a lasting impression so the managers would remember me the next time I called? Not an easy thing to find, but I knew there had to be something. I can't tell you how many hours I spent agonizing about my follow-up, but I can remember the day it came to me because it helped me understand I had been wearing blinders. My solution was right there the entire time.

While serving as a marine, there was a tradition to collect and trade coins. The coins were usually round and came in different sizes and colors. There is an entire culture in the military built around coins, and many marines have beautiful wooden holders to display the coins they've gathered over time. For the most part, coins are given to troops by high-ranking officers or enlisted members. Get one from a four-star general, and you've really got a trading piece in your collection.

The history of the "challenge coin" goes back to WWI when a squadron commander had a coin made for his pilots, each of whom wore the coin in a leather satchel around his neck. One pilot was shot down and taken prisoner by the Germans. He eventually escaped and made his way to a French outpost where he was detained again. His new captors didn't believe he was an American because many impersonators had been infiltrating Allied camps and the pilot's ID had been taken by the Germans.

When the pilot realized he still had the leather satchel and coin, he showed the coin, and the French officers saluted him, gave him a bottle of champagne, and sent him back to the American front. This started the tradition of units and generals casting and presenting coins to the troops. When I thought about creating a coin of my own to send as a follow-up to FAs, I quickly dismissed the idea as crazy and said to myself, "Who am I to have a coin made? I was never a general or a sergeant major."

It wasn't until I took the blinders off before I realized that I was no longer in the military. If I wanted a coin, who was going to tell me I couldn't have one? The coin became my signature, my lasting impression, and people remembered me because of it. It was perfect because it was specific to me and my background. One side had the markings of a drill instructor, and the other had the flag-raising over Iwo Jima. With every coin I mailed, I included the history of the coin on a handsome tissue paper insert. And I always included this handwritten note on the accompanying card:

> *If you're ever in the company of a marine or a group of marines, show them this coin, and you will be welcomed into a long-standing tradition that has been celebrated for decades.*

I sent this coin to many managers and FAs in my years traveling the country. There would be times I would need to return to an office, and I would notice my coin sitting on the manager's desk. I once had a great talk in Arizona with Chris Johnson, the author of extremely well-done workout books and a fine motivational speaker. I gave him the coin in person and followed up with an e-mail about the history. Take a moment to read his response:

> *David,*
>
> *I'm sitting here writing my next book and your coin is staring me right in the face because it's sitting on my computer. It was great meeting you and I look forward to our next encounter.*
>
> *Chris*

I was recently presenting in Dallas for a financial advisor trainee program. A young lady ran up to me after the presentation and said she didn't realize who I was until I started talking about the coin. She told me that she was in her mentor's office every day, and while there, she always played with a coin the older FA kept on his desk. That, of course, was a coin I had sent to him three years earlier. Think about that: years later, my coin still sat on his desk as a reminder of our meeting. Now that's a lasting impression.

What's *your* lasting impression? Equally importantly, how much time have you spent thinking about it?

Advisors rationalize their reluctance by saying, "Yeah, David, that stuff is great, but we just don't have that kind of time to devote to it." My answer is a throwback to my days as a drill instructor: *bullshit!* You have the time; you just aren't making the time available.

For years, advisors asked me to write their value propositions for them. They pleaded, they begged, they said they didn't know where to start, and I could do it so quickly, and all their troubles would be gone. I bet you figured out my answer: "I'm on the road 110 nights per year. How in the !#@$#%!$@# world could I possibly write the bio for every advisor who asked? There are sixteen thousand of you at Merrill Lynch."

Truth be told, I could have written their biographies while logging all those miles in the air. During my five hundred thousand miles with Continental, I watched every episode of the *Sopranos*, *24*, other TV shows, and lots of DVDs. Could I have been writing biographies? Yeah, I had the time, but I just wasn't about to make the time. It's all about where the marketing falls in an FA's priority list. How important is it to you? If it's important, make the time.

Remember the test with the client's daughter going to college? And how low the percentages were? Now imagine that same client calls and says, "I have $2 million you didn't know about at another firm, and I want to move it to you in September. Can you call me in two months to make that happen?"

In this follow-up test, how many FAs do you think actually schedule a follow-up for two months later? How many will put a giant Day-Glo

Post-it note on their wall or do something to remember to get that $2 million?

Which of the two scenarios is most important? Getting that money in two months or the child going off to West Virginia? Most FAs are adamant that it's all about the $2 million, but it's not; they have it skewed. If you can perform well in the college scenario, if you go deeper with your clients by saving and using the data that is staring you in the face, you will get many more second scenarios, whereby clients move more assets to you because you are exceeding their expectations in the relationship.

Both scenarios are *equally* important, and as soon as you realize that and buy into that way of thinking, you will start to make time for the little things, the follow-ups, the lasting impressions, and the system for capturing and mining data.

Don't Forget to Cover Expectation

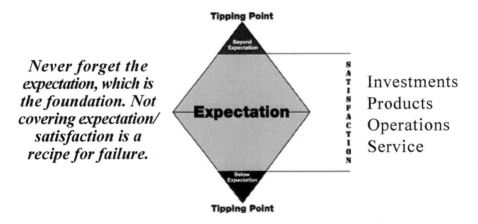

Never forget the expectation, which is the foundation. Not covering expectation/ satisfaction is a recipe for failure.

Investments
Products
Operations
Service

At this point in my training programs, someone invariably asks, "Are you saying the middle of the diamond is not important and we should just focus on the relationship?" Absolutely *not*. I would never tell you that the middle piece is not important. In fact, the middle (investments, products, operations, service) is the foundation and expectation and cannot be overlooked, forgotten, or executed halfway. You must at least cover expectation and satisfaction, and then you can start playing at the top.

If you try to bypass the absolutely critical expectation and go straight to the tipping points, you will ruin all the work you did on the tipping points and, most certainly, lose the business. Here's an actual example of what can happen when a company misses basic expectations and goes straight to the top.

JetBlue

I was enjoying my platinum status with all the upgrades that went with my Continental mileage program. Continental has a reputation for exceptional service to business travelers, and I measure and judge them every trip I take. In August 2010, I had to take a trip to Utah and fly home from Las Vegas on my own dime. I searched diligently for the cheapest fare since I was traveling with my brother and paying for both tickets. I'm very loyal to Continental, but I wasn't willing to kick in the extra bucks it would take to stay with them for this flight; loyalty only goes so far.

I booked a flight on JetBlue Airlines. I had heard all the bad press about them due largely to their extremely long takeoff delays. When I boarded, I was surprised to see televisions built into the seat backs. My expectation was a normal drop-down TV for which, unless you're positioned perfectly, you need binoculars to watch. Many airlines are upgrading their technology, but Continental seems to be doing it one plane at a time.

The "personal" televisions definitely went beyond my expectation for an airline that prides itself on being affordable. The next very pleasant surprise came when I realized that all the monitors had live TV—and it was free. Free! Are you serious? Continental charges all non-first-class passengers for their two planes that have DIRECTV. But here on JetBlue I can flip through channels like I'm on my living room couch, and I don't have to pay a dime for it.

Beyond expectation? Absolutely. Enough for me to tip and leave Continental? Not yet, but they certainly made an inroad. The final straw came when the flight attendant announced that all JetBlue flights offered Dunkin Donuts coffee onboard. *What*! Nothing in this world makes me happier than a cup of Dunkin Donuts java. My ritual every morning is a gym workout followed by a trip to DD for a large steaming hot coffee in the winter and iced coffee in the summer. My DD coffee with just the right amount of cream and sugar is simply ecstasy.

Now JetBlue hit a tipping point. My own monitor, free live TV, and my favorite coffee. Would I leave my long relationship with Continental for JetBlue because of those amenities? Absolutely! Remember, everyone has his or her tipping points, and that was enough for me; I'm leaving and taking my business to JetBlue. You can't argue with the logic. It's my decision, my tipping point. I own it, so it doesn't have to be logical.

Sitting in my airline seat and visualizing my new life as a JetBlue frequent flyer, I couldn't help but think about how brilliant JetBlue was. Whether they knew it or not, they took airline coffee, which has an expectation of terrible, and found they could exceed their customers' expectations just by offering a better brand of coffee. Brilliant. It reminded me of P. F. Chang's when they first launched their new restaurants. My brain automatically put them in the Applebee's/Chili's category for dining. My expectations were exceeded as soon as I pulled up and was offered valet parking. What a great way to communicate that you are better and more sophisticated than the Applebee's of the world. They built a more sophisticated brand and are able to charge more than middle-of-the-road restaurants by creating a better atmosphere and more sophisticated experience.

As the flight attendants made their way down the aisle, I'm actually overwhelmed (honest!) with anticipation. Seeing actual Dunkin Donuts cups on the serving cart made me feel as if I was home even though I was flying at thirty-five thousand feet and still thousands of miles from my family. When the flight attendant reached my seat, I talked her into giving me two cups of coffee (you never know if she'll be back!). I applied just the right amount of cream and sugar and anticipated my first sip.

Here's a question for you: what was my expectation for this coffee? Think about that carefully because it's extremely important for this lesson. Was my expectation that it would taste like Dunkin Donuts coffee? You bet. I was pleased that they served it, but the coffee still had to cover expectation, which in this case was the taste. It was terrible, probably the worst coffee I ever drank, and worse than regular airline coffee. Tipping point ruined. Everything else JetBlue did to get my business was ruined because they couldn't cover the expectation of coffee taste.

Do not forget the middle piece! You must have product, you must have service, you must have advice, and you must have an operation that will show you to be a well-oiled machine capable of managing someone's life savings. You are the one who will keep your clients happy during their retirement. You are the one who will ensure they have enough income to stay retired; you are the most important person in their lives when it comes time for retirement and planning for it. Your job is that important.

A side question for you: If I would have left for JetBlue, would Continental know? Would they reach out and ask why? Would they look for me? Would they care?

At least 99 percent of the FAs who were asked that question responded with a loud *no*. Continental would not be aware that I left. What do you think? Many feel that they wouldn't know because they don't care, but I disagree with that. I'm a Platinum flyer, and someone in that company would care if I left and went to the competition. The only reason I believe they wouldn't know or ask me why is because they don't mine their own data. They don't have the right alerts in place to watch customer tendencies and put rules in place when behavioral anomalies appear. They also don't have processes in place to understand and study why their customers are leaving nor do they know how to share that data across their businesses.

How do I know what I'm talking about? I test everything, so I tested Continental, Marriott, and Avis in early 2008. I had the top status with all three and wanted to test my theory of how poorly they all mine their data. I already knew Continental didn't do a good job with data because I watch them carefully. I'm amazed that their flight attendants aren't trained to review their passenger list—which has the status of every flyer—and simply thank Platinum members for their loyalty, which would take about five seconds. Imagine being a Platinum member, sitting on a plane without an upgrade, and the flight attendant approaches you and says:

> *Mr. Smith, on behalf of the captain and Continental Airlines, we would like to thank you for your loyalty as a Platinum member. Once we're airborne, the captain would like to offer you a complimentary drink from our menu.*

How long does that take? Would it make you feel special, different, part of the family? You bet it would. And it would also stop me from leaving for JetBlue because of TVs and Dunkin Donuts coffee. Unfortunately, that type of culture must be bred from the top down. For you as a financial advisor, you're in the driver's seat because you get to decide the culture for your business and your book.

> *Do you see the opportunities in the data?*
> *When you do, make sure you seize them!*

PS: In the span of 2 years, I shot up to Platinum status with Marriott and Continental. I flew over 100,000 miles a year and stayed in over 200 hotels while renting a car from Avis every time. When I left all three to do my test for 6 months, none of them called me. I ended up staying with Hilton and never went back to Marriott. It's now been three years, and Marriott still hasn't called me to inquire why I left. When I left Avis, I went to National and loved the fact that I got to pick my own car from the lot, so I stayed with them too. Avis never called and will never know that the only reason I left is because I wanted to pick my car. I stayed with Continental only because their hub is in Newark, 45 minutes from my house and flying other airlines was a pain. My conclusion is that all three companies are throwing good money thrown down the tubes. Not smart business for them, but you have every opportunity to make your business smarter. Exceed expectations.

Notes

Notes

Notes

Notes

Notes

CHAPTER 5

THE NINE PROSPECTING METHODS

There is no silver bullet. There is no magic feather. You cannot get your thoughts across to a prospect through osmosis or even prayer. To obtain new business, you have to work for it, and the best way you can do that is to use one or more (preferably more) of the proven, successful nine prospecting methods.

I've worked with financial advisors in every corner of the United States, and I truly believe that many of them are sure there's a silver bullet method to prospecting. They seem certain there's a process, a technique, a system they haven't yet discovered, but they're sure it's there, ready to call on and apply when all else fails.

Well, there isn't a silver bullet or similar imaginary device that's going to make their businesses better. What there *is*, however, is a series of prospecting methods—nine overall—that can be used in various combinations, not to just kick-start a business, but to keep it humming as well.

The real power in prospecting is to combine two or more of the nine prospecting methods and put them to work for you. If you use only one of the methods, I would call you a 1P, which means you make the least effective use of the methods. My hope is that after reading this chapter and adopting the skill set, you will become at least a 4P or a 5P.

The first step to growing your business and creating a marketing plan is to determine which of the nine prospecting methods you plan to use. Prospecting is hard work and mostly about numbers and contacts, but before we get into the nine specific methods, I want you to first ask yourself one question:

How many people today know that you're a financial advisor who didn't know yesterday?

During my live presentations, I'm always amazed—shocked, actually—at the answers financial advisors give to that simple question. The majority of them, most of whom interact with people all day long, usually respond with "zero." I press on, asking them about their day-to-day interactions with ordinary people. Forget prospects for now. What about the clerk at the store where you frequently shop, the person in front of you at Starbucks, the waitress at the restaurant you went to for lunch. Are you telling me that none of them know you're a financial advisor?

Now, you may ask who cares if those service people know what you do; they certainly don't fit your client profile. But I would argue that every interaction and every meeting is practice in communicating and relationship building, and we all know that practice makes perfect. You would be surprised at the connections and interactions you can end up with.

An example of the value: imagine that you're meeting a prospect at the local Starbucks where you had taken the time to talk to and get to know all the employees. Your prospect comes in to spend some time with you and is immediately pleased—feels good actually—that everyone in that Starbucks knows you by name and treats you with white-glove service. What a positive first impression you've made on that soon-to-be client.

I often go to lunch with financial advisors across the country and ask them to take me to their favorite restaurant. When we walk in, I watch how they interact with people in the restaurant. Do other diners or restaurant employees know the FA? Does the FA know their names, faces, or anything personal about them? This visit to a restaurant, an everyday occurrence, helps me understand the level of communicator, connector, and relationship-builder I'll be working with.

Do *you* know the owner of the dry cleaner where you've been dropping off and picking up clothes for years? Do *you* know who serves your coffee, repairs your car, and delivers your mail? You should get to know as many people as you can in a day. I ask FAs to try to meet five people during their travels each day and give each one a business card so each knows what the FA does. Get as much information as you can about those people and keep that information stored in your database as previously mentioned in the Data chapter because you never know when and how you might be able to turn that into a deeper connection.

After asking the important question about how many people know you're a financial advisor today who didn't know yesterday, you then have to ask yourself the more important question: how many days will I answer zero before I realize that my business growth goals through prospecting will never be achieved until that number changes from zero to four every day?

What is your number?

The Nine Prospecting Methods for Financial Advisors

- Referrals
- Networking
- Cold Calling
- Seminars
- Events
- Cold Walking
- Direct Mail
- Local Ads
- Trade Shows

If I had to pick the two most popular methods with financial advisors, I would have to say the answer depends on their length of service. Younger FAs tend to select cold calling and seminars, while seasoned FAs prefer networking and referrals.

One of the great puzzles is that often, when I speak to highly seasoned FAs—men and women who actually built their businesses on cold calling and/or seminars—I find they no longer use those prospecting

methods. Why not? A typical answer is "I did them so well, I stopped."
Strangely, they don't see the irony in that statement, even when business
is slow.

More about that later. Let's review the nine methods and talk about how
you might use each one to drive new business to achieve your growth
goals for the year.

1. Referrals

This method is crucial to *any* business. Every financial advisor should not
only incorporate this prospecting method into his or her selling toolbox
but also build structure and planning around it. I like to break referrals
into two separate buckets—*clients* and *centers of influence*—because
there are distinctly different ways of handling each group.

Clients

I've spent time with thousands of FAs throughout the country, and the
majority of them do not have structure around how they seek referrals.
FAs tend to look at their book, find their "best" clients—those who have
invested all their assets with the FA—have a great relationship with the
FA, including the spouse, children, basically a big lovefest—and think,
That's the perfect client to ask for a referral.

But what if that "best" client is an introvert or an analytical personality
type? Would that client still be a good referral source? Actually, *no*!
We know that the analytical people don't make good referral sources.
And being a great client doesn't offset the limitations of someone's core
personality.

One day I'd like to do a study that takes the question of analytical
referral sources to another level. We know that the analytical personality
type doesn't like to give referrals because that study has already been
impressively concluded in a book called *Pathways to Higher Education*
and many other studies on personality traits. What I want to know is how it
makes this category of client feel when they are actually asked for a referral.
My suspicion is that they probably don't like to be asked, and I would

further assume that it might also make them feel uncomfortable. Why do I make that assumption? Logic tells me that if someone doesn't like to do something, they probably don't like to be asked to do that very thing.

So if being a good client doesn't make for a good referral, what does? It's the *personality type* that's the key, not the amount of assets you control or the sophistication of the client's portfolio. Malcolm Gladwell, in his book *The Tipping Point*, talked about three personality types:

- Salesmen
- Mavens
- Connectors

The "salesmen" types tend to be people who "sell" their ideas on others, who want to get people to agree with them. The "mavens," as Gladwell describes them, are information specialists, often "people who want to solve other people's problems." But when I read the section on "connectors," everything came into focus for me. Malcolm doesn't highlight this type because he thinks they would be a good referral source. That's not what his book is about. I realized immediately that connectors are the perfect personality type for advisors to use for referrals. And once you read what follows (and may I suggest you purchase a copy of *The Tipping Point* for yourself), you'll probably find that you and many of your colleagues are connectors.

A connector is someone who loves to put two people or groups of people together. Here's a perfect scenario: An individual approaches a connector, who may be a friend or a colleague. The individual says to the connector, "Hey, I'm taking my wife to the new Italian restaurant that just opened downtown. Have you been there yet?" The connector immediately comes to life and says, "Wait, I've got a good friend who manages the place. I'll make a call and get you a great table. Give me ten minutes."

As promised, the connector returns in ten minutes with positive news: everything has been taken care of. The individual is to go to the hostess, give his name, and he and his wife will be treated like visiting royalty. It's important for you to understand that connectors do this because there's something in it for them, no matter how intangible it may seem. (We all are aware of WIIFM or "What's in it for me?")

And what does the connector get from this? A connector will spend the next couple of hours thinking about the couple experiencing white-glove service at the restaurant. A connector will derive joy and pleasure from making the connection because that's how a connector is wired. A friend, acquaintance, or coworker has a need? The connector will work to find someone with a solution.

I was in a Merrill Lynch office a few years ago and did a morning group presentation, followed by one-on-one meetings throughout the afternoon. As part of my morning opening, I mentioned that I brought my son with me because we love to travel to different baseball stadiums every year—and this year, it was the town in which I was working. I told an amused crowd of fifty advisors that leaving a fifteen-year-old boy in a hotel room with access to room service and movies for $10.99 a pop was probably not the smartest thing in the world to do, but hey, it's a guys' trip.

A few hours after the presentation, I was walking down a hallway when an advisor ran out of his office and flagged me down. He asked what I was doing with my son that night since our game wasn't until the next night. I told him I didn't have any specific plans, but we would probably go to Dave and Buster's, a chain restaurant known for large rooms filled with kid-friendly video games.

He said he was working on something and asked if I could come back to see him in a couple of hours. Curious, I said I would and went back to work visiting different FAs. When I returned later in the afternoon, the FA who had stopped me in the hall produced two fifth-row tickets, complete with a parking pass, to the professional preseason football game for that evening. I couldn't believe my luck.

This FA was a classic connector. There really wasn't anything I could do for him that I wouldn't do for every other FA I worked with, and for that matter, he never asked me to. Yet I'm sure he had a joyful evening picturing my son and me enjoying a night of football and bonding that he made happen. As a connector, it would make him feel tremendously happy to know what a blast we had that night.

Connectors can be the key to a successful referral program, but first, you have to find them in your book. They don't always have the most money, but once you know what to look for, they're not that difficult to identify.

They simply love to be known, and it is important for them to know others simply because it's part of their DNA. They're the ones who are never intimidated by meeting new people and are happiest when they're attending various functions. Actually, according to Chi Chi Okezie, owner/ producer of SIMPLEnetworking, LLC in Metro Atlanta, Georgia, it's commonplace for them to host or sponsor events. They have heightened networking awareness and create networking opportunities. In general, they enjoy the spotlight and are always eager to expand their network.

Once you identify your connectors, the next step is to make sure they can connect you with your ideal client. It's such a waste to have connectors who can't put you in touch with affluent people.

I'm a great example of a connector who tends to be overlooked. I assume the advisors in my hometown never ask me for referrals because they must think I'm the poster boy for Ameritrade or Charles Schwab—it must seem to them that I don't have enough assets to be viable. However, I'm extremely connected in my town, which you'll see in the networking portion of this chapter. More importantly, I'm networked with affluent people who would make perfect clients.

I'm not upset or offended by the omission, just curious and intrigued by it. And it's helped me realize that advisors spend too much time asking for referrals from the wrong personality types. Wasting time trying to get referrals from, say, an engineer who's a great client doesn't make much sense if he's an analytical introvert. Don't overlook the less-affluent individual who has the personality traits of a connector and can guide you to your ideal client.

Once you've identified your connectors, put a plan into practice about how best to ask them for referrals. But you need to be careful of landmines that can blow up in your face. For example, telling a client you're working on increasing the number of clients in your book can be translated to mean, "Uh-oh, my FA is going to get bigger and have less time for me."

Another example of a landmine is what I call "bait and switch." When you ask a client to come to an event but front-load that invitation with the "feel free to bring a friend," I want you to understand something. Your clients are not dumb; they realize what you are doing. They know you want them to bring a friend to your event because you're hoping to convert that friend into a client. So don't try to mask your intentions because it diminishes the power of inviting the client to the event in the first place.

I'll cover more of this challenge in the events segment, but be aware that there really are better ways to ask for referrals from connector clients. Here's an example: take the client to dinner, tell her you are moving some of your clients to a more self-directed platform because you can no longer spend the time required on their small accounts. This, of course, will free time to add clients who are more like the connector client you are treating to dinner.

Now you can feel secure in asking for help with introductions to friends, colleagues, or family members who would be a perfect match for the kind of client you specialize in. If the client is truly a connector, he or she will go to work on your behalf. It's that simple. Constant follow-up with the connector is imperative because connectors are often somewhat disorganized and overinvolved in too many projects—which is part of what makes them good connectors in the first place.

Have a plan for what kind of a gift/reward you will send to a connector client whenever he or she provides a referral and something even better if the referral actually becomes a client. I recommend dinners with the connector as this helps to strengthen the relationship and reinforces your plan to increase referrals through your connectors. Pay close attention to the Gifts chapter because it can help you create the perfect gift and experience for your connector clients as they flood you with referrals!

Centers of Influence: Community Leaders, Attorneys, and CPAs

This is a much more difficult referral source. Clients tend to already trust you; after all, they've given you their valued assets to invest and manage. That doesn't automatically make them a referral cakewalk, but centers of influence are in a far more difficult league.

Think for a moment about your favorite client. To make it crystal clear, this is the client you would be distraught over losing.

Now, imagine going to a Starbucks or whatever your favorite coffee or snack place might be, and you run into a CPA you know from the area. You chat for a while and agree that you could probably help one another. During your conversation, the CPA learns that you have a client who the CPA has been trying to meet and bring on as a new client for over a year. The client the CPA is referring to is that same client I had you bring into focus, your best client.

My question to you is how long would it take before you would feel comfortable referring your best client to the CPA? What kind of relationship would you need to build before you would refer your best client? How many contacts? How many lunches? Would the CPA need to refer business to you first? How deep would he have to go to get that referral?

I've asked that question thousands of times. The answer varies, but the theme is always the same: it would take over a year, many contacts, and a deep, deep relationship. But that was true a couple of years ago, before the market meltdown. Now you can double the time required.

Why so long? Trust has been rocked in the financial world, and it's a bigger gamble on the part of the COI to refer a good client to a financial advisor. You are asking someone to give you the name of a client who continues to put food on their table, money in his children's college savings account, and contributes to his 401(k).

So to get the referrals from COIs, there's a lot of work to do. The average contact with these referral sources averages three times per year. Not enough contact to build a long-lasting relationship with trust as the foundation. This kind of contact requires more than just sending an electronic newsletter or e-mail once a month. There are numerous dinners, holiday parties, lunches, golf dates, special events, and whatever else you can offer throughout the year. From the time you get a COI referral source in your crosshairs, don't expect to see the benefits for more than a year, and that's only if you work the contact on a regular basis.

One of the issues with centers of influence—largely attorneys and CPAs—is that they tend to be analytical personality types, which makes it much more difficult to get a referral. And there may come a time when you simply have to cut them loose. I've seen too much time spent on COIs who will *never* offer a referral.

Give yourself two years. If you've been working a COI for that long without gaining a referral, you've made the right amount of contacts throughout the year, even referred them business, and yet received nothing in return, cut them loose. Move on and look for other COIs who may be more accommodating. There are plenty of them out there, and you need to use your time wisely.

As for contact with the COIs, I've seen some interesting and unique methods in my travels around the country. During one tax season, I ran into an FA who sent a gift basket to all his CPA "partners." He put a big stuffed bull (symbolizing the Merrill Lynch brand) in the center of the basket and lined the outside with Red Bull drinks. He filled the middle of the basket with No-Doz stay-awake caffeine pills and included a note: "I know you're burning the midnight oil during tax season, so I thought you could use a little help. I'll call you when things slow down, but I'm thinking about you."

Isn't that great? The FA reinforced that he valued the relationship and demonstrated how much he knew the CPA, understood his business, and what was going on in his life. *Bam!* That's a contact!

Here's something else to think about. You've worked diligently to find quality COIs and craft good relationships. If these attorneys and CPAs gave your brochure or marketing piece to their clients, how would they deliver it when asked if they can recommend a good financial advisor?

Not ideal: "Sure, I know a good financial advisor, in fact, I know a few of them—here are their brochures."

Ideal: "Actually I have a good friend who is a financial advisor. Here is his brochure, but I would like to set up an introduction. This is a great person who I would recommend to my own family members."

Obviously, the second scenario is the one you are driving toward, but it takes time. Don't rush the relationship because (1) if you push too hard, you could lose the contact and (2) when the referrals do start, they seem to flow like water from a pressurized fire hose. Younger FAs often try to close too quickly and end up ruining their brand and any possibility for a referral. Build the relationship naturally.

2. Networking

This is a very broad method and tends to be the most unstructured of the nine prospecting methods. Networking is a long-term strategy that can take years before you start reaping the benefits. At some point, however, you *must* ask for the business or, at the least, ask to do a financial checkup for the people with whom you've been networking.

The best producers I've ever met drove home this point over and over again: *don't be afraid to ask for the business.*

You should begin networking by putting structure around the process and being certain you are networking in the right places, attending the right events and sitting on the right boards to accomplish your mission. I know you probably have networking in your business plan, but when was the last time you asked yourself the following questions about your networking activities:

- How many people am I meeting?
- How many events am I being invited to because I'm on the board?
- How many events do I attend where I'm introduced as a board member?
- How many relationships is this activity allowing me to build?
- How deep are the relationships I've built?
- How many people have I met through my existing networks that are now clients?
- How many prospects from my networks have I added to my pipeline?
- How much time is this taking?
- Am I doing it to give back to the community or grow my business?
- How many new networks have I tapped into because I'm on this board?
- How many events do I plan to go to this year?
- Who will be at these events?
- What networks will these events tie me into?

All these questions are vital to a successful networking program. Yes, I called it a *program* because anything less than that is unstructured. I want you to build structure around *everything*.

I'm constantly looking at FAs' business plans, and I'm immediately drawn to the networking part of the plan. Sure, it looks good in the business plan: You're going to grow your business by 15 percent, and you're going to do it through referrals, seminars, and networking. It certainly pleases your management since it looks as if you have a plan in place to grow. Managers always love that. Unfortunately, when I probe with questions about networking, about 90 percent of the conversations go like this:

Coach: *I see you have networking as one of your methods for growth next year. Let's talk about that. Where are you networking?*

FA: *Well, I'm on a couple of boards, and I'm going to attend some galas and events.*

Coach: *OK, let's talk about the galas and events first. Which events have you gone to previously and exactly which events are you planning to attend throughout this year?*

FA: *I haven't gone to any yet, and I'm working to find some that I can go to.*

Coach: *That's great, but unfortunately, it's June, and you put this in your business plan in December. It looked good when you typed it, on paper you have a great plan for the year, but almost half the year is gone, and you haven't gone to an event yet. You need to not only make a list of every event you plan to go to when you create your business plan, you also need to identify why that event will help you grow your business. How many of your perfect clients could be at the event, what's your plan and goal, how many people do you need to meet for success? How are you going to follow up with them? What are you going to mail them to leave a lasting impression?*

FA: *I hadn't thought it through that far.*

Coach: *Let's talk about your networking on boards. Which ones do you sit on?*

FA: *Well, I haven't actually been to a chamber of commerce meeting in months, and I just left two other boards. At the moment I'm really just on one board, at the local YMCA.*

Coach: *OK, let's talk about the YMCA board. How many people are on the board?*

FA: *Ten.*

Coach: *Ten including you?*

FA: *Yes*

Coach: *OK, how many people on the board would make good clients? How many are clients? How many are prospects? How many have you asked for the business? How many have you asked to do a financial checkup? How many have you offered a financial organizer? How many community events are you getting invited to because you're on the board? How many people are you meeting because you're on the board? How many YMCA marketing pieces carry your name because you're on the board? Are you on the YMCA local Web site listed as a board member? How many people come to the board meetings and see you acting as a board member?*

FA: *Whoa. Hold on a minute. I really do this because I want to give back to the community, and you're making it all sound impersonal, structured, and strictly business.*

Coach: *Yes, I am, and I'm doing so because you included networking as a growth method on your business plan. When I asked how you were going to network, you told me through your boards and events. When I asked about events, you didn't have anything specific. When I asked about the boards, it came down to the YMCA. And when pressed for answers about how that board will help you grow, you give me a speech about giving back to the community.*

There is nothing wrong with community-minded volunteerism. It's the backbone of America. And where you choose to spend your personal time is no one else's business. But I have a problem when you put it in your business plan and don't put structure and measurement around it. If you're doing it to give back to the community with the hopes that maybe, just maybe, someone will give you business, take it out of your business plan because it just doesn't belong. If you're truly using networking to grow, then ask the right questions and put structure and measurement around it. (More about that in the Marketing Plan segment later in this chapter.)

Networking is all about extending your brand recognition through interactions with people who have networks of their own and who can introduce you to other networks. No matter where you go, always ask yourself how many people you met, how you can turn them into clients, and how you can get them to introduce you to their networks.

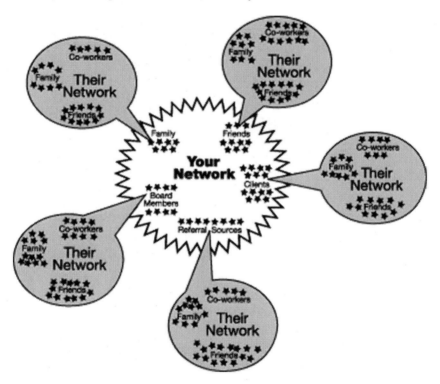

I ran into an FA once who created his own personal networking system. He used an Excel spreadsheet and listed all one hundred plus of his clients. Whenever the advisor had a conversation with a client and heard the client mention a name, he added that name to the client's row with a follow-up reminder. The next time he talked to that client, the advisor would mention the person's name from the last conversation and ask for an introduction.

Can you imagine what that spreadsheet looked like now that he's been using it for over five years? Sounds overwhelming, but to the FA it made perfect sense. I loved that he could gain a client and trace that client back to a referral he got from another client two or three years earlier. It showed how intertwined people actually are and how closely connected the networks are.

I try to put to practice anything and everything I'm recommending. Some of my book is marketing instinct, but a lot of it is experience. For networking, my experience came just after moving home and separating from the Marine Corps. One of my goals was to network within my community and get to know people.

What was my motivation? I wanted to become the mayor of my hometown. I had a vision of going to my twentieth high school reunion, and after all the doctors, lawyers, and CEOs boasted and bragged, I would make my own grand announcement: that's great, guys, but I'm the mayor of this town!

I knew that to actually make that happen, I needed to get to know people and build my networks. Little did I know I was going on a journey that would be my training ground for helping thousands of FAs network properly.

If you want to get on a board, have a plan.
I knew I wanted to get on a board that was appointed by the mayor, and I didn't care which one. I just needed a starting point. I went to the public meeting held by the town council and sat through the most boring meeting of my life. When it finally ended (seemed like ten hours!), I introduced myself to the mayor and explained that I had been stationed all over the country as a marine and had come back to my hometown to raise my family. I went on to say that I wanted to be involved in my town and asked if there was some kind of board position or committee I could be appointed to.

The mayor very graciously thanked me for my civic interest and explained that all applications for boards and committees should be mailed to the "Mayor's Talent Bank." With that, he gave me a firm political handshake, a pasted-on smile, and a quick exit that was so smooth I didn't realize then that I was being brushed aside.

I went home that night, put together a bio, and mailed it first thing in the morning. And then began the wait. After two weeks, I began to get a little antsy and went to the next meeting, reintroducing myself to the mayor. I filled him in on the steps I had taken and followed-up by attending several more meetings over the next few months.

I became a stalker. I would not allow that wall to be erected in front of me. I would achieve this mission if I had to take that wall apart brick by brick. Finally, the mayor caved in and appointed me to a position as an alternate on the Zoning Board of Adjustments. *Zoning board, what the hell is that?*

I had no idea what I was getting into, but in the five or so years I was on that board, I learned a lot about zoning. More importantly, I met about 50 percent of the business owners in town and lots of attorneys and residents. Whenever a controversial case would come in front of the board, many people would approach me in the community, saying they saw me at the board meeting.

This was a perfect example of networking. It was exactly what I was trying to accomplish. I was meeting people, extending my networks, tapping into new networks, interacting with new people, and building great relationships the entire time. Even business owners I had voted against for some kind of variance would end up becoming friends or acquaintances.

One such applicant was a father and son who were embarking on a new ice cream retail store. They were seeking a variance to reduce the number of parking spots required for their business. With the exception of another board member and me, the rest of the board was fine with the variance.

Now I'm not an engineer like many of the other board members, so I used a common sense approach. I knew the ice cream shop would be swamped over the summer, and I worried about customers parking across the busy street and having to navigate the street, often with small children in tow.

I asked why the father and son wouldn't simply use the adjacent lot they owned for overflow parking. They responded that they wanted to sell that lot and use the money to help finance the ice cream shop. Well, I disagreed and voted no. I lost the vote, but that didn't stop me from building a wonderful relationship—a true friendship—with both the father and son. I got to know them through the zoning process, and three years later, they sponsored my daughter and gave her $1,000 to participate in an educational trip to Europe. You don't have to allow a disagreement to deteriorate into an adversarial process. When you do, you get the kind of animosity and gridlock that has become so much a part of our political system. Nobody wins.

Another zoning encounter was with a resident who wanted to build a two-story pool house. I was confused by the plans and couldn't get a handle on what they were doing. Two-story pool houses were strictly forbidden in our town, so why were we even listening to this case? Turns out the reason I was confused was because the first story was actually underground. The first floor started one story down, so they could have a swim-up bar; people in the pool would be eye level with people on the first floor of the pool house. It was really lavish, with a gorgeous bar, big-screen TV, you name it.

As an advisor, do you think this would have been a good client to have? Absolutely! But here I was, asking this person tough questions about the plans, the noise, the impact on his neighbors. As we began the vote, I joked with the resident and said I'd vote *yes*, but I wanted an invitation to the first party. Sometime after the vote—a win for the resident—I ran into and asked how the pool house was coming along. He said it was finished and extended an invitation.

This individual is still a friend today, along with the mayor, committee members, numerous affluent residents, business owners, and attorneys. The networking paid off and did exactly what I had wanted it to do: extend my reach and my brand.

Last point on networking: there are board positions that are simply not right for networking. After my time on the zoning board, I was promoted to the planning board and then offered a spot on the parks and recreation board. This board was very prestigious; we managed a large budget and did great things in the community. But remember the original goal? It was to network and build relationships along with my brand.

With this new board, there were ten people in a room once every three weeks. We had lots of power within the community, but there were no other people in the room when we met. No press, no residents, no business owners, no one. While this was a great board to be on to give back to the community, it was not helping my mission at all. Ultimately I dropped that board because the time commitment and my dream of becoming mayor was put on hold until the kids grow up but the lesson is to constantly evaluate your networks to ensure they are supporting your overall goal.

How many people know you are a financial advisor today who didn't know that yesterday?

3. Cold Calling

This is one of the oldest and most reliable methods for filling your pipeline.

I believe that every manager and every firm should require new advisors to make at least forty to fifty cold calls per day, which, by hardcore cold calling standards, is a mere snack. More seasoned advisors, who have committed to cold calling as a prospecting method, average 100 calls per day. Hard core cold callers I have run into across the country, make 150 to 200 calls per day.

There is a hidden benefit to cold calling that many people don't realize. It first occurred to me when I started to role-play with new trainees. I sat them in a room and asked about their value propositions and what made them different from everyone else. In a matter of minutes, I was able to pick out the cold callers. I knew because most cold callers were able to nail their value propositions on the spot with no preparation and without even thinking. Once I fully comprehended that, I began to probe deeper into this method to find out what the successful cold callers were doing, how they continued to work in this prospecting art form, and still navigate the growing Do Not Call list. Here's what I learned.

Keep your eye on the mission.

The mission is *not* to sell a product or get a new client, which can be an overwhelming task in this new world of distrust. The mission *is* to get the contact to agree to a five- or ten-minute meeting. And to meet at a location that is easy to get to yet sophisticated enough to meet the contact's expectations of where he or she might feel it would be appropriate to talk about investing.

That means McDonald's, Wendy's, and Burger King are out. I would approve of something called Joey's Crab Shack *only* if it's a monument in town, a place that all locals know, love, and respect (even if it is a dump). If you stay focused on just getting the meeting, you will find the task much easier and the call less sales oriented.

I ran into a financial advisor who made his way through the very difficult Merrill Lynch trainee program in record time. This is not an easy task. In fact, there have been times when the failure rate in this program was over 75 percent. But this particular FA—a cold caller—did it with ease.

What was his secret? *Data.* He would target a company and use a mailing list broker to rent or purchase a list of employee names, titles, and work numbers.

If you can't get hold of that kind of list, then do what another resourceful twosome did: they created their own directory for the company they were prospecting. These two fireballs called 411 to get the main company phone number (almost always available now via the Internet).

The number was something like 888-555-1000. They knew that every company used sequences to assign phone numbers, so they started calling 1001, 1002, 1003, et al., until they had an entire company listing with names and phone numbers. Brilliant!

So back to the hotshot advisor who obtained the company directory. Before he made his first call, the advisor spent weeks researching the company, their compensation model, and 401(k) plan. He looked for information nuggets; things many employees might not know (e.g., whether to do a distribution or a reinvestment). Once he found a nugget, it was like ringing the cowbell for dinner. He would locate an employee hangout—either in the company building or close by—and conduct his meetings there.

The cold call conversations were easy and productive. And they went something like this:

Hi, I'm — with —, and I've worked with some of your colleagues at — company. I'm not sure if you know this, but there is a distribution you can take with your 401(k) prior to the end of the year that could be beneficial for you. What I did with your colleagues is reinvest that money into . . . Would love to meet you, buy you lunch at —, which is right in your building, and talk about how I might be able to help you.

That simple conversation worked like a charm. The trainee built his book and rocketed through the program.

Stay away from scripts

I'm often asked if I have written scripts to share with FAs. The answer is *no*. I hate scripts. The problem is that if you are using a script, you sound *scripted*. I don't care how good you are; reading from a script makes you sound as if you're reading the words instead of feeling them. I think a script becomes a crutch.

Honestly, you don't need a script. What you need is experience, repetition, and bullet points highlighting those things that make you different, that give you reasons why someone should do business with you. Think about the objections people hit you with, and come up with reasons that show why the objections are invalid. Focus on the positives.

There are three ways you can attack objections:

> *Avoidance.* This is the way most FAs try to offset objections, but it is the most dangerous method. By avoiding objections, you never have the opportunity to address them. And if you don't address them, you will never gain the respect you need to grow your book.

When working with young FAs, I ask them how they plan to address the fact that they are young. Why should someone do business with them when there are hundreds of experienced FAs who have been in the business for ten or twenty years or more?

Most have no idea how to answer this question, but they agree it's something their prospects are thinking. And the young FAs handle it by not handling it. They avoid the question, they never get their say, and they never get to argue their merits.

Waiting. FAs tend to know what a prospect or client may be thinking, but many prefer to wait for the prospect or client to address the issue. I found this to be the most practiced technique following the purchase of Merrill Lynch by Bank of America.

I role-played with FAs: "Why should I do business with your company? Didn't Merrill Lynch almost go out of business? How can you ensure that it will never happen again? How do I know my money will be safe?"

Every FA knew this question was paramount in people's minds, but most FAs were afraid to address it. Instead, they waited to be asked the question. The problem with this method is that a prospect or client may never ask the question, or if it's finally asked, it might not be framed in a way you're ready to answer.

Think about being prepped to go through surgery, and you ask your doctor how he can be sure you will live. What if he hesitates or flubs the answer? Does that give you confidence? Do you think there's any difference in your relationship with a prospect or client? You are supposed to be the trusted advisor, and you must breathe confidence and be prepared to answer any objections, especially the tough ones.

Attack. This is my preferred method. And it has nothing to do with my military background. But it has everything to do with taking charge.

When I started traveling the country for Merrill Lynch, I knew that FAs would view me at first as a "home office puke" or a "talking head". I could practice *avoidance* and pretend they weren't thinking that. I could *wait* and hope they'd get to know me in time and eventually accept me. But both methods would only keep the FAs in shutdown mode and not open to my suggestions which, of course, were in their best interests.

I needed to attack their objections and have my say. I went right at them with statements like, "I know I'm the home-office guy and we have not always made it easy for you to market yourself, but I'm here now, and I'm fully committed to helping you grow." I needed to build their trust, and to do that, I needed to let them know I knew what they were feeling. Home office people were perceived by the field to be merely "punching their ticket", meaning, traveling the country and listening to FAs but never following up with changes.

Nothing came out of my mouth in a presentation that was not thoroughly thought through with the "cynical FA" in mind. What would a twenty-year veteran think? How could I best go right at his or her objections?

When Merrill Lynch launched its *Essential Partner* marketing campaign, we highlighted FAs and their sensational relationships with clients. I had to present this new campaign to the field, but before I jumped into it, I went through the likely objections, the most glaring of which would be: "This is nothing new, we've had these relationships for years, and where have you been?"

My plan was to go right at that objection before I said one word about the new campaign: "I know you have built beautiful relationships with your clients, and this marketing campaign is nothing new. What's new is that we're simply realizing this is what makes us different as a firm, and we're going to market that fact." This disarmed the FAs because my response was on target. They knew it, I knew it, and the home office knew it. Sometimes it's the way you approach things that makes all the difference in the world.

The technique is to *attack*. Go right at objections before they even come up. Are you a young FA? *Attack*. Say to that tough prospect, *"I know you're thinking I'm young, but here are the reasons why my youth will be extremely valuable to you . . ."*

Cold calling is about *numbers*. The more prospects you go after, the better your chances are at getting meetings. When I'm working with cold callers, I try to get them to reach at least 100 calls a day. The more calls you make, the better you get at doing it.

I marvel at the conventional wisdom of some of the new trainee programs on Wall Street and why cold calling isn't considered mandatory.

I would gather groups of seven to ten trainees and start role-playing. I would ask why I should do business with them, what makes them different from everyone else, and how they can assure me that my money would be safe with them. I'd hammer away with questions, and then after approximately ten minutes, I would stop. With approximately 90 percent accuracy, I could identify the trainees who made over one hundred cold calls per day. They were quick on their feet and were able to answer my questions without hesitation and with the confidence necessary to be a financial advisor.

All cold callers will tell you the same thing: you must do the numbers if you expect to be successful. And I'll attack any objections you have to this method. Seasoned FAs, older FAs, often see cold calling as a step backward in their career. To them I say, "Get over yourself, you're a salesman." Cold calling is a great way to fill your pipeline, and it *works*.

You have to make time for this method and make the calls. And while I'm in attack mode, don't talk to me about the dreaded *Do Not Call* List. There are millions of potential investors who are *not* on the DNC; there are plenty of numbers for you to call, so stop using that as an excuse. Get out there, and get some business. The more excuses you find, the higher the wall you're erecting between you and new clients.

4. Cold Walking

This is definitely not a method often used by the FAs I've encountered, and I've worked with thousands; it seems to be a dying prospecting method. I've only met one FA who cold walked residentially. I think he was from Edward Jones, which practices this method much more than the likes of UBS, Merrill Lynch, and Morgan Stanley.

However, there are some things you can do that will help you be successful with this method. Virtually all cold walkers go to businesses to meet and greet. The most effective way to do this is to bring information that is specific to the industry in which you are cold walking. Going in with, "Hi, I'm a financial advisor, and I would love to spend a few minutes talking about how my firm and I can help you with your portfolio, 401(k), and your personal finances" is basically lame.

That approach is so generic, and it's been done thousands of times. Why be generic when you don't have to be? With cold calling, you aren't sure what you have on the other side of the phone. With cold walking, you know *exactly* whom you are approaching. You research the industry, get relevant reports, market trends and specific problems that the specific industry is facing. And then go in with solutions, not with a generic pitch that has absolutely no meat.

Walk into that doctor's office with a purpose and an answer to the most pressing financial issues doctors are facing. Talk to them about how you've helped their colleagues, and explain some of the methods you used. Leave them with marketing material that is specific to their needs, not a generic fact sheet about you and your practice. This is the most successful tactic when using the cold walking method.

Cold walking is not an approach for a timid or lazy person. Understand that there is a lot of up-front work before you make your first stop. Research the industry, and plan your route in advance. Most FAs just get up from their desks and start walking the busy streets. I'm not saying this won't work eventually, but I am saying it's not the best use of your time.

Additionally, you will need to get through the "gatekeeper" at most businesses. I've found two methods to accomplish this task. The first is pure salesmanship—charm the heck out of that gatekeeper. Build the relationship, and you'll find unbridled access to the decision maker. It's a beautiful thing.

The other method is "sneaky" but very effective. Beat the gatekeeper to the building. Get there before the gatekeeper arrives, and you'll find that the decision maker is unguarded and access can be achieved. What you do with it depends on how well you did your research and what kind of compelling argument you've crafted as to why the decision maker should do business with you. If you do use the "sneaky" approach, make sure the decision maker gives you an introduction to the gatekeeper before you leave. Then build that relationship to ensure access remains intact.

Cold walking is a numbers game that takes a lot longer than cold calling. It can be extremely effective if used properly. The more you do and the better you plan, the more your pipeline will grow.

5. Seminars

If you asked me to name my favorite prospecting method, there would be no contest. Seminars are, by far, my premier choice; if I were an FA, this is exactly how I would build my business. That said, you have to understand that seminars are also a numbers game. The more you do, the more prospects will fill the pipeline and the more likely you are to convert prospects to clients.

There are some best practices you *must* follow if you are going to use this method. These are not negotiable: you have to do all four of the following without fail. These best practices have been the difference between successful seminar programs and failures.

> *Create a Twelve-for-Twelve Seminar Program*
> Notice that I used the words seminar *program*. That's because one or two at a time won't cut it. You need to develop a program that approximates twelve seminars over twelve months.
>
> I'm "amused" (annoyed, really) when I talk to FAs who tell me that seminars didn't work for them. When I ask how many they

ran, the response is usually two or three. *Are you kidding me?*
If I said cold calling didn't work because I called fifteen people
and none of them wanted to meet me, you would laugh me out
of the business.

For some reason, FAs think of seminars as a higher calling, a
much more sophisticated way to prospect as compared to cold
calling because they're face-to-face with prospects. But guess
what? They're wrong: seminars are still a numbers game, and
the more you do, the better your chance of success.

If you plan to do one seminar, then, based on its success or failure,
decide if you are going to continue to do more, I have a message
for you: *quit now*! I'll save you the time and effort and tell you
what will probably happen at your first seminar: the room might
have twenty people in it if your topic hit home (see "Seminar topic
must hit home" segment later in this chapter). And if you're doing
a seminar that includes food, you can be sure that approximately
ten of the twenty attendees will be *plate lickers*.

Plate lickers, as mentioned earlier, are the people who come to
your seminar to eat your food but have no interest in your message
whatsoever. They plan dinners around seminars and consider you
the meal ticket for that particular afternoon or evening. Of the
remaining ten attendees, four of them will probably be existing
clients with another FA from your firm, particularly if you are
with a large firm like UBS, Morgan Stanley, or Merrill Lynch.

Of the six left, four will run up to you after your seminar and talk
your ear off. Later you'll discover that these eager beavers had
no money to invest and were excited to get an unexpected and
undeserved invitation to your seminar. What they did do was eat
up much of your relationship-building time.

The last two attendees either left before the end of the seminar
or politely waited until the second it concluded. Those two very
quiet attendees were probably the ones with the investable assets.
And if you don't use the "follow-up" best practice described
later in this section, you will never get those accounts.

Your seminar program must be a complete commitment. You *must* do one seminar per month for twelve months. At the end of the twelve months—and assuming you pay attention to the three best practices that follow—then and only then should you assess whether or not your seminar program is working for you.

Plan for one seminar; plan for twelve seminars. By that I mean never put one seminar through compliance; put the next six in. Never reserve a room at a hotel for one seminar; reserve six months' worth. Never print one set of mailing labels for direct mail invitations; print six copies of the labels. This kind of thinking needs to be part of your program for the next twelve months. If you execute the seminars as a program, you will find that month 6 has particular significance. This is typically when seminars begin to evolve into a process and become much easier to execute. This is when it all comes together.

You'll understand what compliance is looking for. You'll know what each wholesaler's process is for helping fund a seminar. You'll be able to get invitations in the mail more easily and manage your RSVPs more efficiently. In month 6, you'll go from "doing" the seminars to "living" the seminars. And that's the point at which I see many FAs adding an extra seminar per month, taking their seminar count to twenty-four per year. Whether you do twelve or twenty-four, you will fill your pipeline with prospects. It's only a matter of numbers now.

You Must Be a Good Public Speaker
This best practice is almost always overlooked, and I don't understand why. Take it from someone who has conducted over a thousand seminars on various topics. It's *not* about the content; it's about your *delivery*.

The power of a seminar doesn't rest on slides, charts, graphs, or standard deviations. The power comes from your ability to inspire and capture the imagination of a group of people. Share your intellectual capital, show how much you are motivated to help, and be passionate and breathe confidence with every word that comes out of your mouth. That's the true power of a seminar.

If you cannot get up in front of a group of people and deliver your message in a way that truly captivates the bulk of your audience, you should not be doing seminars. Does that statement make you angry? Do you disagree with what I'm saying? Well, so be it. I'm speaking from experience, and I can tell you it's all about your delivery at this stage of the prospect relationship.

Let me go a little further: if you're afraid of speaking in front of a group, if public speaking has always been an issue for you, the bad vibe—the fear—will pour out of your body, and you cannot hide it. If you *can* hide it, you're a public speaker, and that's simply how it works.

I've taught many people how to speak publicly, including new marine drill instructors. Talk about hazing: we used to hand a book of Marine Corps history to a new DI and throw him out in front of a group of three hundred recruits. Go ahead, we'd say, teach these recruits about WWII and woe is you if any of them fall asleep.

With absolutely no preparation, these newbie DIs would be forced to get up and teach history. They had to have confidence because what good is a marine drill instructor with no confidence? It was one of our most effective hazing rituals, and it worked very well in quickly getting the DIs to (a) feel comfortable in front of a group and (b) understand how to inspire the group. If their delivery—or yours—is effective, the information will make its way into the minds of recruits or prospects. If your delivery falls short, they will turn you off quicker than you can blink your eyes.

Let's talk about fear, which is what you project if you're uncomfortable with public speaking. You can't hide the bad body language, the stammering and stuttering, the image of someone who's timid, nervous, and not confident. What is someone with a huge portfolio and an apprehension of a volatile marketplace going to think as he or she watches your performance? "Oh yes, that's my financial advisor, the timid and scared one up there. That's the one for me." I don't think so.

Many FAs will revert to what they are comfortable with: the markets, standard deviations, product, and economic trends. They bore their audience silly and miss the opportunity to inspire confidence.

Perhaps you're one of the many FAs who think you're smart by asking a wholesaler who is an awesome public speaker to step in and do the majority of your seminar. That's not smart at all. I've spoken with hundreds of wholesalers who have told me stories of how the FA cowered in the corner as the wholesaler executed a flawless seminar. What do you think happened after the seminar? People approached the high-performing wholesaler wanting the wholesaler to be their financial advisor.

What else would you expect? The wholesaler did exactly what the seminar speaker was supposed to do. He or she was inspiring, shared impressive intellectual capital, and breathed confidence into the minds of the audience. The FA? Well, what did the FA do other than introduce the speaker?

You must be a good public speaker to make a seminar program work. If you aspire to be a better public speaker, get a coach, practice often, and have someone attend your seminar who will give you good, honest feedback on your performance. Videotape the seminar so you can view it later and do a postmortem with your coach.

I've coached many an FA, and one of the best ways they can improve is to find causes in their communities for which they can volunteer and speak in public. Many years ago, I found a perfect opportunity for myself when I was forced to attend a three-hour certification course at Rutgers University for people who wanted to coach a variety of sports.

Attendance was state mandated, and the people who conducted the seminar were not the best speakers. Three hours of utter hell. I thought that this could be a great opportunity to keep my own skills sharp and to kick the certification course up a notch with a presentation that would keep coaches engaged, informed, and entertained. In other words, *inspired*!

Like I said, it's not about the content because I used the same slides as all the other people running the clinic. But the feedback from the evaluation forms was very different for me. In fact, a nearby town refused to use anyone other than me for their twice-a-year clinics. And do you know why? *The delivery, not the content.* Look at the schools in your area, volunteer your time, teach young kids how to invest and save money. Every opportunity is a good opportunity. Public speaking is like a golf swing: use it or lose it.

Your Seminar Topic Must Relate to Your Invitees
An FA I'd been coaching recently told me he was concerned about his seminar program. He had conducted a mix of cold calling, direct mail, and local ads to get people to come to his seminar. Even though he was diligent about the process, he didn't receive a single response. No one so much as bothered to RSVP.

He was annoyed and asked me how it was possible that he could do everything right but not get any attendees. In response I asked him what topic he had selected, and he said it was exchange-traded funds, ETFs. Frankly, I couldn't think of a worse topic for this particular time. Here are the major concerns of Americans—affluent or otherwise—right now:

- Healthcare
- Retirement
- Safety of assets
- Social security
- Market volatility
- Value of real estate

No wonder no one wanted to come! Did the FA's topic have to do with anything that's top of mind with an audience? The issue isn't about having a seminar about what *you* think people should be concerned; it's about offering a seminar that addresses *their* concerns.

Look, you're asking people to give you their time. They need to leave their houses or jobs and give you at least one or two hours of their time, and it better be about something that concerns them. Yes, of course, ETFs could be a great thing for affluent people to learn more about; ETFs could even help them address one or more of the six major concerns I just listed. But first, you have to get them in the seats. The seminar topic must be directly relatable to what concerns your audience at the moment.

Here's another example that might hit a little closer to home. If I were planning to conduct a seminar series for FAs to help them understand how important building and executing a marketing plan can be, do you think I would send an invitation with the title: *Learn How to Build a Marketing Plan?* Would you disrupt your busy schedule to come to a seminar on that topic?

Don't bother answering that question because I know the answer. And that's why I would never dream of sending a seminar invitation with that title. I would sell the *benefit* of the seminar in the title, something like: *Learn How to Drive More Business and Double Your Pipeline in Twelve Months.*

Will I talk about the need for a marketing plan in the seminar? Absolutely. But I'm not going to lead with it in my invitation because it won't motivate you to come. Always, always, always remember that what is important to you may not seem at all important to your prospects. By offering a key benefit in the title of the seminar, you can help prospects understand the value of what you have to say.

Follow Up for Twelve Months

This is the crucial step, but it's often not done well. Many FAs simply don't put in the work that makes the follow-up pay off. It's hard to believe that an FA will go to the time, trouble, and expense of conducting a seminar but not do proper follow-ups.

During the seminar, for example, you *must* get all the contact information you can on your attendees: name, address, phone number, and e-mail address. You need to make this mandatory for every single attendee. *Require it!*

Make sure you manage attendee expectations by telling them at the seminar that you will follow up with them by phone to answer questions. The first call is when you will qualify them as potential clients, understand their needs, capture as much data as possible, go for the one on one and/or explain your method of contact for the remainder of the year.

You must "drip" on these attendees for twelve months, with at least one contact per month (the average is two contacts per month). Maintain a constant drip, and have a process in place to keep you on track. The only way to build a deeper relationship with prospects is through contact. The more you have, the deeper you go, the more standard the contact, the less effective it will be so make sure you use your data effectively.

My advice to you is to make twenty-four contacts per year, per prospect. Twelve of them can be automated—for example, a newsletter or research report—but the other twelve should be personal, such as an event invitation, a birthday card, phone call, face-to-face meeting, or other activity.

Don't forget, the name of the seminar game is *numbers*. Conduct a steady stream of seminars, and you will build a pipeline of prospects.

While the four seminar tips just offered are crucial, there are a few other thoughts I'd like to pass along. What follows won't be defining factors in your program, but they can definitely enhance it:

Surveys, Yes or No?
You're attending a seminar or class, and the person conducting it says, "It's survey time! Before you leave the room, please complete the survey form so we can deliver an even better experience for you." Does that proclamation give you a good

feeling? Do you say to yourself, "Oh boy, it's survey time, my favorite part of the day."

You know the answer. Virtually everyone hates to do surveys. So what's my point? Why in the world are we closing out a perfectly positive experience with a negative one? FAs who do surveys always jump on me for that comment: "Well, David, we need to know if the seminar was good, if the food was good, if the place was comfortable, the topic engaging. We need to know!" My response to these survey gurus is "You should be following up with a phone call to every attendee, and while you have them on the phone, *ask them those same questions!*"

I will not do a survey. No one wants to answer them, so why end a program negatively? I'll tell people that if they have feedback, they can bring it to me after we break or during the phone call I promise to make to them within the next few days. Don't do anything negative. Keep the seminar experience totally positive!

In fact, I'd go beyond that. I would market the fact that I don't do surveys with a statement like this in my closing remarks: Folks, I know at this point in a seminar most people pass out a survey. I don't do that for two reasons: one, no one likes to do surveys and two, I'm going to follow up with each of you by phone. If there is something you want to share with me, I look forward to hearing it during our conversation about how all this information applies to you, your life, and your portfolio.

That's the way to close a seminar!

Location
Lots of FAs have seminars in their offices mostly because it's easier and cheaper than going to an outside facility. But think about this: it's a fairly safe bet that a good prospect has an existing FA, and it's one thing to ask that prospect to come to a neutral, nonthreatening site but quite another to ask the prospect to come to your lair/office. Coming to your office requires a much higher level of commitment than coming to a neutral location.

You could be losing prospects and not even realizing that it's because of where you're asking prospects to come for an event. And then you need to take a hard look at the location of the seminar. Is it really sophisticated enough to send a message about your brand and the kind of high-level work you do? I've seen FAs have seminars in their local YMCA. And, frankly, I don't think that kind of location is suitable for a sophisticated advisor to have their seminar, always keep an eye on your brand.

Breakfast? Lunch? Dinner?
Should your seminar include lunch, dinner, or breakfast? That's a very difficult question to answer because there are many variables I would need to know. If, for example, you were conducting a seminar in Florida for retirees, 7:00 p.m. is probably way too late. If you work for a prominent firm like Merrill Lynch, UBS, or Morgan Stanley, you need to serve a sophisticated menu because the expectations will be much higher due to your brand. Let's just say pigs in a blanket probably won't fly (even though they are so damned good!).

One tactic you can use is offering dessert instead. I love this method for a couple of reasons. There is no question about what's being served, and if dessert is advertised, it puts attendees on notice that they need to eat before they come to the event. I've seen many seminar invitations say that appetizers will be served, but inevitably, attendees leave disappointed (and hungry) because they expected to fill up on bite-sized hors d'oeuvres.

Dessert can be sophisticated, and yet you can keep costs low. You can also add wine and cheese to a dessert menu, which also raises the level of sophistication. And, finally, dessert will keep away some of the plate lickers, many of whom will not sit through a seminar just for dessert.

A warning: you will get fewer attendees because of the time of night coupled with the fact that it's "only" dessert. But the crowd you attract will be much more dedicated and interested and not distracted by the missing plate lickers.

If you are prospecting employees of a specific company, you might be interested in what I've seen some FAs do with seminars. First, they run the program very close to the company's office and combine it with a lunch or a happy hour. This works great because lunch doesn't take away from the employees' time at home and happy hour is minimal time away. I love it!

Best Practice Highlight: At the end of a seminar, the FA offered attendees the option of ordering dessert to go, so they could bring something home for their spouse, a nice way of saying, *"Thank-you for your time and the family time you gave up."* I thought this was a classy move, which was appreciated by the attendees.

Best Way to Get Prospects to Your Seminars
The most effective way is a 5P process, cold calling, networking, referrals, local ads, and direct mail. Using a combination of all these methods is the best way to get maximum numbers of attendees to your seminar:

- Utilize your network to inform people that your timely seminar hits one of the top concerns for Americans.
- Utilize your clients and COIs to obtain referrals or ask them to attend and bring someone who might be interested.
- Use cold calling to shift your mission from trying to get a five- to ten-minute first meeting to asking people to come to your seminar. This is also the most cost-efficient strategy since the 5P process comes with a high cost for local ads and direct mail postage.
- If you plan to do direct mail and local ads, make sure the ads are in carefully targeted publications, and the direct mail is sent to only affluent neighborhoods you want to pinpoint.

I recently ran into a young trainee who was going broke by mailing invitations every month to up to three thousand households. She did it right, though: she followed-up every invitation with a call, and that's where she sealed the deal. I like this method because your opening statement can be, "Did you get the invitation I mailed you?" However, she couldn't afford to keep doing it, and I told her to dump the mailing. If you can't afford the cost of a mailing and you're following up with a call anyway, just go right to the call, and come up with a good opener. It worked out just fine for this FA.

One final thought about seminar invitations. When I ask advisors how much time they spend on the invitation, I would have to say the average is one hour, and that includes writing, reviewing, proofing, approving, and time spent talking about design and content. The next question is how much time is spent on the outside of the invitation, also known as the envelope.

Average answer? *Zero.* I think you should spend equal time working on the outside as you spend on the inside. Remember, your envelope has to make it through the clutter of daily junk mail. If your envelope has the generic, standard/stock computer-generated envelope look with the address printed and a number generated in the address field, it's as good as garbage.

I analyze my own reaction every day as I go through the mail, and I've been doing that for years. I pay attention to what immediately gets through, and then I document why. I also document why some pieces go straight into the trash. Over the years, I found that any letter with a stamped address on it goes into the trash immediately. Most seminar invitations don't make it through, but I will share with you one example of an invitation that did.

The advisor partnered with a well-known local restaurant. On the front of the envelope were the words "A special dinner invitation from Nona's." The return address on the front was Nona's, and the back flap had the advisor's name and contact info. It passed through my defenses because I immediately thought my local Italian restaurant was having something special. I thought it was brilliant, and more importantly, it got through the clutter. I wonder how much time that advisor spent designing the outside of his invitation?

How much time do you spend?

Don't forget the Clemenko golden rule for seminars: the purpose of a seminar is to educate; the power of a seminar is to *inspire*!

6. Events

One of the biggest mistakes I see is the common FA practice of combining seminars and events such as having a dinner with a speaker or a wine tasting with a presentation on tax minimization strategies.

The way I look at it is that events are good for relationship building, and seminars are good for educating. But combining the two absolutely does not make either one extra powerful—it actually dilutes the positive impact.

Before you toss this book into the circular file, let me explain. There are many, many times I've witnessed a wonderful wine-tasting event where the execution was flawless. What made it so? A look around the room told you everything you needed to know. *Relationship building* taking place everywhere: clients talking with each other, the FA/team interacting with everyone, attendees having a great time. But, more importantly, the FA is gathering data, data, and more data.

And just as the evening of good feelings is reaching a crescendo, the sponsoring FA interrupts everyone with the *buzzkill* announcement that Bob from Blank Mutual Fund Company is now going to talk about tax minimization strategies. *Noooooooo!* He is stopping the very thing at which the event is wildly succeeding—interaction, relationship building, the dismantling of walls and barriers that are allowing you to learn more about everyone in attendance.

Why the !#@$#%$^#%@$!! would you stop that happy flow, that evening of fun and good feelings, with a presentation? If you want to educate people, do it with a seminar. If you want to build relationships, do it with an event. If you combine the two, make sure you have planned for plenty of relationship building time.

Here are my best practices for creating outstanding events:

Feeder Events
Some of my colleagues at Merrill Lynch hated when I used the term "feeder events." To them it meant a food event even though I said repeatedly that it had nothing to do with food. It was all about process. Feeder events are not about feeding people; they are about feeding from your pipeline to the next stage of your contact strategy.

Like seminars, events need to be part of a strategy, and an event is one step in an FA's overall contact strategy. You meet a prospect, the prospect attends your seminar, you follow up with a call, and you start gathering information to assess if the prospect will be a good client for you. And then you feed the prospect over to your upcoming event.

You should *always* have an event on the horizon because you should have one schedule for every other month. Just like seminars, you must have events on a regular basis and get them all on the calendar in the beginning of the year. This organizational process, for some hard-to-figure reason, seems to be one of the toughest things for FAs to do.

I know that most FAs consider it a huge ordeal to put on a large event—usually a client appreciation event—and when it's over, they are exhausted and don't even want to think about another one for a year. I want you to break away from this unproductive thinking and do what's best for your practice. Find a good venue, and book six events on the spot. Get them on your calendar, and pay for them in advance, and you will be amazed and delighted at how they fill up and become successful.

Keep it Small and Intimate
Once you have your events scheduled, keep each one to twenty people, ten couples. This is important because that's how you'll manage six of them throughout the year. You don't need printed invitations because all invitations should be done over the phone. Prospect (or client) confirmations should be done through e-mail,

texting, or whatever communication form makes your invitee most comfortable.

I once worked with a team that needed to visualize everything; they hated putting information inside what they called "the Box"—their computer. They felt that once the data was in there, it became unnoticeable along with the million other bits of data that were never seen or heard of again.

We brainstormed a while, and I came up with a plan for them. We put six flip charts on their wall—each with an event date at the top—and numbered one to twenty on each one. The idea, of course, was to start filling in their events as they talked with prospects. If during the contact phase they believed a prospect could be a good client, the prospect was invited to the event. As people accepted, their names—husband and wife, partners, friends—were written in the next available numbered spots. As one event was filled from one to twenty, they moved to the next chart. This helped them stay on track, fill each event and, more importantly, remind them when an event was approaching and wasn't filled.

This is the feeder process, the act of feeding your prospects to the event as part of your contact and relationship-building process. The events should be small to give you the ability to build relationships with the ten couples you have in the room. Don't get into the mind-set that you'll have one big event and get it over with for the year. You are the person who binds all the attendees together, and you are the person with whom they'll want to spend time, and vice versa. Keeping it small means you can gather good data.

Think about a wedding you've attended. How much time did you get with the bride and groom? Were you disappointed that you didn't have more than a couple of minutes to chat? It's no different with your client-appreciation dinner. If there are fifty clients, how much time can you actually spend with each one? Not enough! Keep it intimate, and ensure the setting is conducive to getting to know more about your prospects and clients.

Build the Ultimate Home Field Advantage with Attendees
Hey, it's your event, so why shouldn't you stack the deck in your favor? I'm often asked what the perfect mix of clients and prospects should be at an event. My answer is that every single attendee should have a purpose. *Assuming all will bring a spouse, partner or friend, here is my perfect mix of twenty people:*

- *Three prospects*
  People you've already prequalified and are pretty sure would make great clients because they have the proper investable assets for your book and are interested in moving to a new FA.

- *One cheerleader client*
  Someone who you know *loves* you and will sing your praises to other attendees.

- *Two referral sources*
  One CPA and one attorney with whom you are trying to build deeper relationships and get more referrals. *Do not* invite more than one of each because the additions would be their competitors (or may be perceived as being so).

- *Two growth clients*
  Clients who have some assets placed elsewhere but you think you have a shot at getting those assets transferred to you.

- *One referral client*
  A connector client from whom you would like to start receiving referrals; this is part of a deeper relationship-building strategy that will allow you to approach this client for future referrals.

- *One center of influence*
  A friend or client that the entire room will benefit from being introduced to that night. A celebrity in the community, an author, a politician. The objective is to increase your brand sophistication; you want attendees walking away saying, "I had no idea he/she knew that person, *wow*!"

Once you have gathered this mix, you become the Great Networker at the event, introducing everyone to each other. You are the individual who binds them all together. You are the emcee, the host, the glue.

When I worked with the events group at Merrill Lynch, I was struck by the impact of the networking that went on between clients at our events. One client would be introduced to another at a dinner, and inevitably, they would find they had something in common, personally or professionally. Either way, long-lasting relationships and friendships were germinated, and they never forgot that the FA was the person who brought them together. Very powerful!

Resist the Parting Gift
FAs love to give clients gifts as they depart from their events. I ask *why*? And my *why* isn't about the gift, it's about the timing.

To me, everything is about brain time. How much time am I spending inside your brain? How much time are you thinking about me? I just brought you to my event and gave you a wonderful evening, so I don't think it's a stretch to assume I'm in your brain.

What I would like to do is extend the amount of time you're thinking about me, so instead of giving you a gift as you walk out the door, I'm going to wait three or four days and mail one to you with a handwritten note. That extends brain time, adds to the amount of time you are thinking about me. This works equally well with seminars and face-to-face meetings. Resist the temptation to give a gift at the door; you get more for your money when you extend brain time.

Cooking Classes and Wine Tastings
Why do I love these two types of events and why are they so successful? Easy. A good sommelier and cooking instructor serves as the master of ceremonies and manages the flow of the event, keeping everyone entertained.

That's important because that frees you to do other things like *data gathering* and *relationship building*! While the sommelier or cooking instructor is doing his or her thing, you can be doing yours. Work the crowd, gather information, and build deeper relationships. Meet the spouses of prospects, CPAs, and attorneys.

If you're having a dinner for twenty people, what do you do with the introverted couple that isn't comfortable talking to anyone? Did you make sure to seat them near you? Or are they all the way at the other end of the table talking to no one? With a cooking class or wine tasting, you don't have to worry about that very important detail.

A wine tasting also allows for a very powerful follow-up, namely the bottle of wine each couple liked best. Both the cooking and wine-tasting venues also offer something a dinner cannot: the ability to walk away with an experience and piece of knowledge the attendee didn't have before.

Other event venues, such as art galleries and museums, offer sophisticated, unique experiences that a simple dinner can't achieve. I once worked with a team that wanted to have a tailgate party before a college game. Tailgating in this town was an art, and college football was a religion. My question to them was, where is the unique experience? Doesn't everyone tailgate? We brainstormed and decided that the unique experience would be having their tailgating party catered by the most popular pub in the town. Now they were onto something!

Bring a Friend, the Old Bait and Switch
Clients are not stupid. When you invite them to your event and then say, *"Bring a friend,"* that's code for, *"I don't care if you come or not, but I really want you to bring a rich friend or relative."* That dilutes the effectiveness of the invitation and assumes clients don't get what your actual intentions are. They're not stupid, and you're making a big mistake if you allow that thought to permeate your relationship. There are better ways to

get a connector client to provide referrals (already discussed in the referral section), and trying to disguise your intentions is not one of them. No one likes to be the recipient of bait-and-switch tactics.

Why I Hate Client Appreciation Events
Hate is a pretty rough word, so maybe despise is a little better. (Probably not, but you get the idea.) My belief is in the mission, but is getting a group of thirty to forty clients together at one venue achieving the mission? What are you trying to do here? Keep clients loving you? Making sure they don't leave? Bolting the back door shut?

Is getting all your clients together for a dinner going to achieve your real mission? Are your clients that shallow that buying them a mass dinner once a year will keep them loyal? I feel that showing your appreciation can be achieved through other methods. Taking them out to dinner in small groups? Yes. Having them for mass dinners? No, thank you.

Events are a powerful way to build on existing relationships, but they're not the be-all and end-all. They're one step or one piece of the overall contact strategy. Events are good for relationship building; seminars are good for educating people, and combining the two makes both weaker.

7. Direct Mail

Direct mail is one of the toughest methods because it will test your patience and your wallet. The industry average for direct mail response rate, as determined by the Direct Marketing Association, has held steady over the years. Here are the key findings of the DMA's 2010 Response Rate Trend Report:

E-mail to a house list averaged a 19.47 percent open rate, a 6.64 percent click-through rate, a 1.73 percent conversion rate, with a bounce-back (bad addresses) rate of 3.72 percent and an unsubscribe rate of 0.77 percent.

Response rates for *direct mail* have held steady over the past four years. Letter-sized envelopes, for instance, had a response rate this year of 3.42 percent for a house list and 1.38 percent for a prospect list.

Outbound telemarketing to prospects had the highest cost per order/lead at a whopping $309.25, but it also had the highest response rate from prospects at 6.16 percent. The highest response rate for a house list was also via telephone, at 10.41 percent.

Paid search had an average cost per click of $3.79, with a 3.81 percent conversion rate. The conversion rate (after click) of Internet display advertisements was slightly higher at 4.43 percent.

Response rates for business-to-business campaigns were generally higher than for business-to-consumer campaigns. Lead generation and high-end average sale campaigns also had higher response rates.

Nearly 60 percent of direct mail campaigns in financial services aimed to produce a direct sale. The average response rate was 2.66 percent for a house list and 1.01 percent to a prospect list. (Source: http://www.the-dma.org/cgi/dispannouncements?article=1451)

So what are the takeaways from this 2010 study?
First, it's disappointing that the study didn't target *only* full service brokerage firms, which means the numbers could be skewed. Having said that, however, the response rate for marketing to financial services prospects was what I would consider a low 1.01 percent. I should note, however, that if you're marketing a high-ticket financial product—such as $25,000 CDs—1.01 percent might be a serviceable number.

I believe that if the study was conducted only for full-service brokerage firms such as Merrill Lynch, UBS, and Morgan Stanley, the number might be even lower. That's because full-service brokerage firms are highly sophisticated, and I don't believe that direct mail is the best method for them to drive new business. But I do think direct mail can be a powerful tool when used *in combination* with a few of the other prospecting methods.

For example, I worked with an FA who wanted to start a campaign to increase his pipeline. We used a 5P method that consisted of cold calling, direct mail, local ads, seminars and events, all within a specific affluent zip code. We rented a list of people, each of whose approximate net worth was one million dollars. This is a more impactful way to target an area and build your brand. When you use a combination of the nine prospecting methods, you increase your chance of success and, at the very least, build your brand recognition.

One of the most common ways FAs use direct mail is to rent a list, make their mailing, and follow it up with cold calls. Most FAs use the same opening line when the prospect answers the phone: "Hi, this is — from —, I was wondering if you received the letter/invitation I mailed you a couple weeks ago?"

Does this method work? Yes? My only problem is with the cost involved. A few months ago, I worked with a very impressive new FA who was eager to build her business. She was spending so much money on direct mail she said it would be impossible to keep going because she would be out of money in a month. Every piece of direct mail was followed by a corresponding call.

I looked the FA in the eye and said, "If you are going to call them anyway, why not remove the direct mail piece from the equation?" She looked at me for a silent moment and replied, "I never thought of that because I love the ease of my opening line where I ask if they received my mailing." This is a classic example of tunnel vision. Wouldn't it be cheaper, quicker, and yes, better to spend some time coming up with a powerful new opening line? Wouldn't it be better to cold call your list without the cost of the direct mail?

Another example of direct mail "abuse" can be found in the lowly postcard. Many young FAs revert to this because it's cheap and easy. My problem with postcards, however, is what it says about your brand. When I work in the field with FAs, I ask them to take the Goldman

Sachs test. I have them look at their marketing postcards and ask if they would expect to receive a mailing like that from Goldman Sachs. The answer is always *no*.

So, I ask, are you less than Goldman Sachs? Is your firm inferior to Goldman Sachs? Do you want to be viewed as a run-of-the-mill, unsophisticated financial advisor? If the answer is no, then I demand to know why the FA is operating like one. Just because you send ten thousand postcards to a great prospect list with lots of investable assets, doesn't mean you will automatically get a response rate of 1.01 percent if what you are mailing is not up to the expectations of the people receiving it. Would you invest a million dollars with an FA who sends you a postcard?

What Every FA Needs to Know about Renting Prospect Lists

First, a little background of how I came to understand the pluses and minuses of list acquisition. About six years ago, Merrill Lynch selected me to go through its Six Sigma Academy to become a black belt. Six Sigma connotes the relentless pursuit of variation. It's not a program or an initiative. It's a way of working and thinking. Merrill leadership created Six Sigma to solve problems for which they didn't have answers.

Traditional Six Sigma follows the DMAIC process. First the problem is **D**efined, then the performance is **M**easured, the situation is **A**nalyzed, and finally, the process is **I**mproved and **C**ontrolled. It may be easier to think of Six Sigma as a big funnel. At the wide-mouthed top are all kinds of potential issues (inputs). By following the DMAIC process, the issues are narrowed as they descend into the funnel. Then action is taken to put into place a plan to improve and control them.

My project was to dissect what happened to people who called the 1-800-MERRILL phone line. How were they treated? What was sent to them in response to the calls? How were they handed off to a financial advisor? What was the process for deciding which financial advisor would get the call? I worked on this project for months and generated a report that rocked the very foundation of our customer service organization.

The calling experience was beyond horrible, and I recommended that immediate changes be instituted.

Part of the problem was that there was no process for prequalifying callers before they were sent to a Merrill Lynch office. Financial advisors were not taking the leads seriously because many of the callers were low income and did not require the services of a sophisticated advisor. I brought in InfoUSA, one of the biggest list managers in the marketplace, to give us list-scrubbing capabilities. Now our call center reps could simply enter the name and address of a caller and the InfoUSA system immediately gave us each caller's approximate net worth, household income, age, and other key demographics. From this data, we were able to correctly decide where to send the prospect, with what degree of urgency, and to determine which follow-up materials would be mailed.

While working on this project, I attained an understanding of how list managers collect data such as household income and investable assets. All data list vendors use is public information. They only have access to public data and nothing else and every list broker has access to the same data. In other words, no one has an exclusive on it, no matter what a list broker may claim. Some FAs rent their list from Experian because they think Experian uses credit score data in their list operation. For the record: they don't, they can't, and it's illegal. For list vendors, it's a level playing field . . . at least until they do their own data analyses.

The vendors hire analytical "data miners" to create reports that spit out assumptions based on the public data. This is important for you to know because the best list vendors are usually the ones with the ability to hire the smartest analytical people. Going to a local list vendor is usually a waste of time. Stick to the big boys like Experian, InfoUSA, and Acxiom.

Another list rental mistake made by FAs is going too low on the demographics. They unknowingly rent the names of people who have way too little household income or investable assets to be of value. I want to teach you the trick for pulling the perfect list.

Of all the data list brokers have, what gives them insight into how much money a prospect has? Give up? It's the mortgage data! The mortgage is the major indicator for investable assets and household income for all list vendors. Unfortunately, the investable assets are often inflated. So here is how you work around that problem: When pulling your list, target an affluent area that you know has a big grouping of your ideal client.

Since the mortgage is the biggest driver in how any income data is generated, you must do the 75% calculation to ensure you aren't pulling lists that are too low in your criteria. In other words, are you sure you are inviting affluent people? If the list vendor pulls a list for you from their database, assume 75% of the assets are coming from the mortgage. So if you were to pull a list in, say, Central New Jersey, a typical FA would tell the list broker that the lowest acceptable household investable assets is $250,000. Now do a 75 percent calculation on that $250,000. And what that tells you is that the low-end group on your list will have a mortgage of approximately $180,000. If you lived in Central New Jersey, you would know that anyone in a house that costs $180,000 is low income. And that means that a significant portion of your purchased list is *all* wrong.

To pull a good list in New Jersey, your asset threshold would have to be one million dollars and above. This would give you a list of people with a house worth approximately $750,000 (75 percent of one million dollars), which should give you the investable assets you are looking for. If you are seeking lower-income families, then just dial back the threshold.

Also, your list vendor should have something called SESI, which stands for socioeconomic status indicator. Basically this is a model that looks at affluence in a household. Use this indicator to help further tailor your list. Use as many data points as you can to obtain the exact client you're seeking.

Example of good list criteria if you're targeting *retirees*:

Zip codes
Approximate Net Worth
Household Income
Age

Marital Status
SESI
Propensity to Invest

And give subscriptions a try. It's great to find people who read *Forbes* and *WSJ*, but if you apply that as a criterion, you could wind up with a list of only ten people.

8. Local Ads

I believe this is probably the most underutilized and misunderstood method of prospecting. The problem is that FAs think that by putting an ad into a publication, they'll have the same results as the local Ford dealer who's pushing for weekend business.

Get that out of your head. Your business and a retail business are entirely different entities. You cannot measure the success of your ad based solely on immediate response to the ad. If you do, you'll probably never run another one. It's human nature to want to put money only into marketing projects that are quickly measurable. But that doesn't apply here. And there's a second problem: FAs usually don't target the proper audience as well as they should.

Let's take a look at each of the two issues, so in your next campaign, you'll know exactly how to use your advertising effectively.

> *Call-to-Action and Response Rate*
> In most ads, you'll notice a very large, very prominent call-to-action. After seeing the ad, we want the reader to respond via a phone number, Web site, or e-mail address. Some ads don't have a prominent call-to-action because the purpose of the ad is to generate brand recognition.
>
> This is where I think the most value lies in local ads for financial advisors. Tone down your call-to-action and reshift your priority from immediate response to brand awareness. Financial services is serious business, and just because someone sees your ad in the local paper doesn't mean that individual is ready to hand you his

million-dollar investment or even $250,000 investment account. The local ad must be part of your overall brand recognition and brand awareness campaign. And it needs to be repeated fairly regularly. For example:

Using a 7P method here, a real full-court press, I'm networking by serving on two boards and attending five events where my target clients are. I'm working through my connector clients for referrals. I'm hosting a seminar a month, one feeder event a quarter, doing some cold calling every day, and I have an ad in the church bulletin. I also sponsor a local little league team, and I have an ad in the business weekly.

I'm not expecting someone to come up to me at the little league games and say, "That's you on the back of their T-shirt. *Wow*, I really need a financial advisor." That would be great, but the reality is that it's just one part of my accumulative campaign. The outcome I'm working toward is for a potential client to see me at an event, recognize me from a board meeting he had attended, know my name because a friend of his attended one of my seminars, and realize that I sponsor one of the little league teams—maybe he even saw me mentioned in the church bulletin.

Don't place an ad with the hope that hundreds of people are going to call because that just won't happen. That shouldn't be the reason you place the ad. But if it's important to you to try to gauge response rates from your advertising, get yourself a brand-new phone number, one that no one else has and that hasn't been promoted anywhere else. Put that number in your local ad, and you'll be able to track the response rate by logging the calls that come from the new number.

No matter what you do, the response rate will be low because that's not where the power of the ad is. And don't be mesmerized by circulation size of a publication unless you do the right calculations. We once put a Merrill Lynch ad in a major metropolitan newspaper with highly targeted affluent zip codes. The circulation was incredibly high, and everyone in the local office was trying to determine response calculations. The problem is that circulation often has little to do with how many people will actually read the ad. To keep it in perspective, if the circulation is two hundred thousand, ask yourself the following:

- How many people are actually reading the paper?
- How many of those readers are stopping at your ad?
- Of those who stopped, how many are interested in your service?
- Of those who have any interest, how many will actually take the time to call you?
- And after someone gets the paper, reads it, stops at your ad, is interested in your ad, and takes the time to call you, there's still another question: is that person the right client for you?

You put that ad potentially in front of two hundred thousand people, but how targeted was it? Keeping your ads in targeted publications will be one of the best changes you can make to your local ad program. And remember, good advertising has a repetitive effect. It builds with exposure. Studies have shown that brand ads often aren't really noticed until the third time they run.

Targeting the Ad

I'm often surprised by how naive FAs are when it comes to ad placement. The answer is as simple as the question: *Where should you place your ad? Wherever your target client is.* If you want to reach business owners in Spokane, Washington, for example, find out what they read and where they socialize. That's how you target your local ad.

If you give me a choice between a full-page ad in the *Tallahassee Daily News* with a circulation of fifty thousand or an ad in a local community newsletter distributed to two thousand people in a retirement community and 80 percent of the retirees have investable assets that would make them perfect clients for my profile, I would choose the little newsletter every day of the week and twice on Sunday.

It's all about targeting your *brand*. Why waste time on people you don't want as clients? It's wasted money to find that the individual you've been working to see only has $1,000 in the bank.

One evening, I was preparing to leave the office and start my weekend when the phone rang. The caller ID showed my wife's cell number, and I guessed she was calling to see what time I was leaving or to give me a chore while I was on my way home. With a travel schedule that had me on the road an average of 110 nights per year and my wife at home taking care of four kids, whatever she asks me to do, I do it and do it fast. This call was no exception as I answered with "Hi, honey, I should be leaving in a few minutes."

She replied with the "wonderful" news that she got a babysitter for the night and that the two of us were going to a show. I had a little trepidation as I asked which show. And here came the hammer: "It's *Little House on the Prairie, the Musical*," she replied happily. Now this was perhaps the last thing on earth I wanted to do on that Friday night, but I performed my role as a husband and replied with what I hoped sounded like excitement. "Honey, that's wonderful. I know how much you love *Little House*, and it gives us a chance to get out together for a night. What could be better?"

She told me it couldn't be better because Melissa Gilbert, who fans remember as Half Pint on the original TV series, was starring in the production and playing the mother. I hung up the phone and noticed my boss looking at me with unrestrained glee. He had overheard the conversation, and I asked him to hit me with his car as we left since that was the only way I could think of to get out of going to the play. He told me it was a tempting offer, but he would rather think about me suffering at the play than at the hospital.

As we walked into the theater—the Paper Mill Playhouse, a very old establishment in the *very* wealthy town of Short Hills, New Jersey—I surveyed my surroundings and looked at the way people were dressed and interacting, and I had noticed a parking lot full of Beemers, Mercedes, and Lexuses on the way in. Oh yes, I was in the midst of real affluence.

I don't know for sure the capacity of this old theater, but I can tell you that if there were five hundred seats in the house, each one was filled with the perfect client for a financial advisor. I also realized they were all doing the same thing at the same time: reading the Playbill, because what else do you do before a show? I thumbed through my own copy to see if any of the Merrill Lynch FAs had thought what I was thinking. But, no, there was not a single ad. The perfect publication with the perfectly targeted audience, and no one thought it might be a perfect idea to insert an ad to show how Merrill Lynch supports the arts.

I'm often asked to speak at Eagle Scout Court of Honor ceremonies in my local community. I talk about American spirit, discipline, and other things meant to motivate new Eagle Scouts. As always, I'm constantly evaluating every venue for marketing opportunities, and I can't help but notice that while the printed program for the ceremony is small and the quality is less than stellar, the room is always packed with affluence and influence. The speakers consist of mayors, town councilpersons, leaders of civic and fraternal organizations such as the Elks Lodge, Knights of Columbus, and Rotarians. Just as with Playbill, this is a way to show your support of a worthwhile program and the community-at-large. Don't pass up these kinds of opportunities!

On the flip side, be careful with what I consider "cheesy" publications. I would stay away from the Penny Shoppers, classifieds, and neighborhood throwaways. You have an image and a brand to build and protect, and they will not help your cause. Some marketers may tell you to stay away from church bulletins too, but I have to respectfully disagree with that bit of advice. Church or temple bulletins demonstrate your commitment to your community, your place of worship, and your faith. There's not only nothing wrong with that; it can be important to potential clients.

9. Trade Shows

This is the method I like the least. And based on my time in the field with thousands of FAs, it's the prospecting method that's used the least. With that said, if you are going to do trade shows, you must consider the following three things: attendees, exhibitors, and the look and feel of your booth.

Attendees
I've run into no more than ten FAs—in the hundreds and hundreds of cities I've visited—who have told me they successfully prospect using trade shows. Interestingly, the ten FAs all went to medical exhibitions, going after highly targeted audiences. Two had booths at chiropractic conferences, three went to dental shows, and the rest targeted medical doctors. Almost all of them spent little or no time at their booths but used the trade shows as networking events.

Think of it this way: a medical trade show brings hundreds of doctors together. Why not mingle in the crowd instead of sitting behind a booth offering cheesy mugs and calendars and looking like a Dairy Queen cashier waiting to ring up the next customer? *You are a financial advisor; you are bigger than that.* Would you select your brain surgeon at a convention booth hawking medical devices? I love to mingle; it's solid, and technically, this falls under the networking method, particularly if you spend little or no time at your own booth.

Other Booths
Watch the company you keep. I can't help but chuckle when walking through my local mall during a show and pass the independent financial advisor who has been placed next to a landscaper or plumber. What do you think happens in that situation? Do you think it brings down the advisor's brand? *Hell, yes*! Seriously, is a craft show really where you want to have a booth? Make sure that wherever you decide to exhibit, your neighboring booths have a high level of sophistication. It will help your overall brand appeal.

Booth Look and Feel

One of the biggest problems I have with the Merrill Lynch trade show booths was the sophistication—actually the *lack* of sophistication—of their booths. Most FAs throw a standard cloth over the table that comes with the entry price, drop a couple of information sheets on it for anyone who cares to stop, and add a Merrill Lynch sign if they were aggressive or thoughtful enough to have one made.

What I ask these advisors to do—and what I'd like you to do as well—is close their eyes and imagine themselves at a car show. Based on who you are, what your company is, and how sophisticated your offering may be, think about which car company you would be if you were there. Are you a Kia or are you a Mercedes? Most FAs should be a Mercedes or a Lexus.

Still imagining yourself at the car show, what would you expect the Kia display to look like? How sophisticated would you expect it to be? What's your expectation for the Mercedes booth? What would that look like? Now think about your booth at a trade show. Throwing down a tablecloth and a couple of brochures isn't getting it done. You need to brand yourself and your booth with the power and sophistication people would expect of a top-of-the-line advisor. You want to attract the right business? You are constantly communicating with your marketing, but what are you communicating when you don't invest in a premium look and feel?

I think targeted trade shows can work if those three methods are flawlessly executed. I would like to see a booth with plenty of branding, a beautiful tablecloth printed with your brand, posters, a designed back wall, and a TV monitor with some clips of panels and seminars. Leave your business cards on the table with your product brochures, and work the room like the networker you are! That's how you make an exhibit work for you.

Remember, if you're at a trade show and the landscapers booth next to you blows your booth away, your booth is all wrong. Lastly, if you find yourself at a trade show that has a landscapers booth, you're at the wrong trade show . . .

Summary

To answer the question of which prospecting method is most popular, I think everyone should do some level of networking and referrals but also understand that it takes a lot of time to see the benefits. I've seen many young and eager FAs fail because they focused too much on their referrals and networking; they didn't give the proper time for the relationships to blossom because they had to hit their numbers, and they tried to close too quickly.

I also believe that referrals have worked so well over the past fifteen years that we have a large group of FAs who are not equipped to go out and hunt using the other prospecting methods. Thirty years ago, many FAs would cold call prospects with a product, a stock, or something to get in the door. This was extremely effective and, yes, it was before do-not-call lists.

These FAs built a hunting culture and were very successful at it. They became financial planners and usually got the IRA rollovers and any other investments their clients had because that generation was blindly loyal. The next group of FAs who came through the system was able to enjoy the benefits that the prior generation of advisors built and didn't have to hunt as hard for the business. Referrals and networking were the staple methods for prospecting new clients.

Now it's a different world, and trust has taken a damaging blow. With that, referrals and networking take twice the amount of time, and FAs are forced to explore the hand-to-hand combat methods the prior generation had to use. You may have to work harder, but networks and referrals offer you the biggest payoff.

Go from a 2P to a 5P, that's when you will see the growth begin!

Notes

Notes

Notes

Notes

Notes

CHAPTER 6

THE MARKETING PLAN

Having a plan is the starting point for any business venture. It's simple, it's basic, and 99 percent of all financial advisors with whom I've worked (out of thousands!) do not have a marketing plan. What bank would invest in a business without a plan? The marketing plan is the partner to the business plan, and it's essential for creating structure to drive new business and retain current clients.

Do YOU Have a Marketing Plan?

As I meet with FAs across the country, I make it a priority to try and understand why they don't have this crucial planning tool. I've found two main reasons, which are consistent everywhere, among young and old, big and small producers, new and senior advisors, and every other variation you can think of. They are the following:

Lack of Time
Most advisors view a marketing plan as they do a business plan: a structured, written document that is five, ten, or fifteen pages. It's what they might have learned at business school or in a freshman marketing class. Or it might simply be a concoction they dreamed up about what a "typical" marketing plan should be.

While I know you're different from every other FA, there are also some commonalities. FAs with type A personalities, for example, have very little spare time, so writing a five- or ten-page marketing document is about as pleasurable as committing hara-kiri. In other words, it's not going to happen. There's simply nothing I can say to type A advisors that would motivate a large percentage of them—and you may be one of them—to sit down and write a comprehensive marketing plan. I'm realistic.

So what's your reaction to this: A marketing plan needs to be a living thing, something that is constantly in motion throughout the year. It shifts with you; it changes on the fly. It helps you stay on track with your business goals, and it helps you drive new business. Throw away your old ideas about what a marketing plan is as I redefine for you how a marketing plan should look and how it's created. Marketing professors be damned, you need something that is actionable and tangible. I don't want you punching your marketing plan ticket.

Ahhhhh, the ticket punchers. Are you familiar with that term? If not, stay with me for a few paragraphs. There was a time when I taught CCD for my local church. To this day, I actually don't know what CCD stands for, but I can tell you that it's church class for young Catholic children. It's generally taught at night during the week, and it requires about an hour every week during the school year. If you want to be a Catholic as an adult, you must first go through CCD from second to eighth grade.

My oldest daughter was in CCD and brought home stories of how the older kids would torment and basically disrespect the all-volunteer teachers. I decided to put on my DI hat and volunteer to instruct the sixth, seventh, and eighth grade kids. I did it for four years, and my first day with each new batch of students always followed the same routine. I stood up in front of the class and said in a very stern tone:

> *If you came here so I would punch your ticket and give you the certificate that Mommy and Daddy want you to have so ten or fifteen years from now you can get married in a Catholic Church, if that's your objective, (long pause for effect) you can get out, and get out right now. I'm not here to punch your ticket, I'm here to teach you. You're not here to get your ticket punched, you're here to learn.*

That usually kept the class quiet, but it was an important line I needed to draw. The question *you* need to answer is, are *you* a ticket puncher? Did you create your marketing plan to impress your manager or are you really using it to drive business? Of the 1 percent of financial advisors who actually do have a marketing plan, about half of them are ticket punchers. They created their plan so they could pat themselves on the back and say to their managers, "Look at this pretty marketing plan I created. Kudos to me."

Can't Answer the Question How?

Think about your business plan. It's very nice, very official, and very polished. A typical business plan will talk about your plans for growth. For example:

> *I plan to grow my business by 10 percent next year. I'm going to do that through two avenues—cross selling existing clients and prospecting new clients. With the cross sell, I plan to reach all my clients with new products they don't have and increase their portfolios and share of wallet. For prospecting, I plan to increase by two households with over $250,000 in assets. I will do this by networking with my local boards and local events, referrals, asking clients and centers of influence for referrals, and I'll do a few seminars targeting retirees.*

Beautiful, great job, says the local manager. You really have great stuff going on for next year, and I can see you knocking it out of the park. But what of the marketing plan? The marketing plan doesn't allow you to get away with pie-in-the-sky b.s. goals. The marketing plan demands that you answer just one question, and that's "How are you going to *actually* accomplish your goals?"

I've torn through advisors' business plans, asking that same question over and over. The answers are almost always less than satisfactory. (Pathetic might be a better word.) I believe the *how* is the most important thing you can answer as you plan your year. And it all lives within the marketing plan.

Here's a conversation I had with an advisor about his business plan. It will be helpful in showing you how to rip apart your own business plan, simply by asking *how*.

This advisor's goals were growth through networking and referrals and acquiring four new households for the year. When I asked him the *how* question, it was clear he would never reach that goal. It was June, and his business plan and goals were almost six months old. He was no closer to the four new households than he was in January, and he was looking for help.

When I ripped apart each of his goals and put it down on paper, he realized that while he thought he was networking, he wasn't. He never put a plan around which events he should go to or, for that matter, how to even get invited to them. There was nothing about how he would turn people he hoped to meet at events into business, how he would drip on people he met at the events, how he would position what he did at these events. *How, how, how . . .*

OK, now it was June, I said, and he had no idea how he's going to meet his goals over the remainder of the year. And what was he doing about referrals, which was part of his plan for new client acquisition? He hadn't asked any clients for referrals nor had he even put any thought around which clients would make good referral sources. He said he thought his clients would call him with referrals even though he had received none during the first six months.

Obviously this shouldn't come as a shock, but why would he get a referral since he hadn't asked for one? If you want the business, ask for the business. If you want a referral, ask for the referral. That advisor will never make his goals if he doesn't put structure around a marketing attack/plan to support his business objectives.

During an event, I made a sketch on a napkin for an advisor I was sitting with. It's a completely different way to approach a marketing plan. It's actionable, it's realistic, and frankly, advisors love it. You don't hear that very often about a marketing plan! That's because instead of writing a marketing plan—an activity advisors seem to find excruciating—I created something to "flow out" a plan. The idea is to keep asking the *how* question.

Start with a blank sheet of paper, and write your goal for new clients for the year. I'm using the number 4 that the FA wanted to acquire.

A New Way to Look at a Marketing Plan

4

Now that you have your number, your goal for new clients for the year, think back to the nine prospecting methods. Writing them down is an important step because you won't bring in any new assets any other way than by some combination of those nine methods. They serve as the foundation for the *how*.

A New Way to Look at a Marketing Plan

Once you put the nine prospecting methods and your numerical goal on the sheet of paper, circle which of the methods you plan to use for the year.

As you can see in the next drawing, which demonstrates your plan for seminars, you begin flowing out how you plan to execute each method. This is a huge step for you because once you have it mapped out, you have actionable take-aways or to-dos to ensure that you continue to follow through on your business goals. This new look for a marketing plan isn't rocket science, and it's definitely doable in a short amount of time.

When you finish this book, I'd like you to add three things to your wall:

1. A piece of paper with "the Number" that indicates how many people know you're a financial advisor today who didn't know it yesterday.
2. A marketing flow chart that matches what we just talked about.
3. A contact strategy flow chart that will be covered in the next chapter.

Here is how the seminar portion of your marketing map should look when it's completed:

A New Way to Look at a Marketing Plan

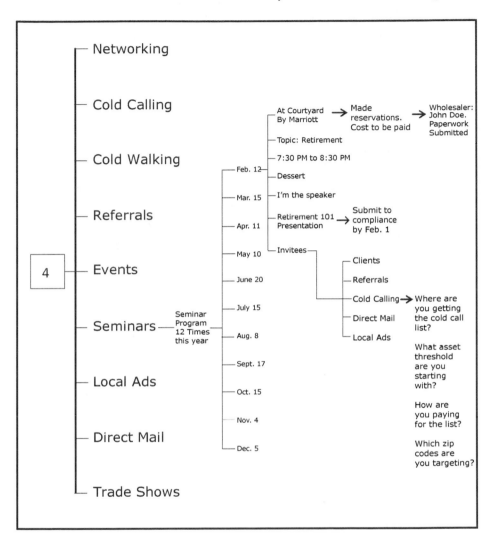

If you continue to ask the important *how* question for each method, you'll find that this method will *force* you into showing critical details, leaving you with an execution plan. Nothing is completed until all the answers have been given.

Case in point: cold calling is a method this advisor will use to get people to the seminar. So what's the next question? Who are you going to cold call? If the answer is a vendor list, the next question is, which vendor? And the answer to that could be Donnelley InfoUSA. Where will you start the asset threshold for your list? $240K. Which zip codes do you want? 00000 and 11111. Will you have any special list requirements? Yes, retirees and preretirees, anyone fifty-five and over, as well as a SESI Code (remember from Direct Mail chapter) of ninety or higher. How often will you cold call this list? One hundred per day from January 15 to February 8.

Now that the cold calling stream is finished, go buy the list and execute your plan for cold calling. I sat with a team, and we flowed out their plan for hours. As the flow grew and grew, three things were painfully obvious:

1. They had never gone into this much detail for executing their business-growth goals.
2. The detail needed to execute their goals is why they came up short every year.
3. They had too many things going on. They were a 7P and could not give the time needed to be successful. I paired them back to a 5P, left their office with the walls covered in flip chart paper, and they ended up having a great year.

Remember, if you don't put a plan around your goals, you can't execute to your fullest potential. What will you be tomorrow, a 2P or a 5P?

Notes

Notes

Notes

Notes

Notes

CHAPTER 7

YOUR VALUE PROPOSITION

What do you do?
What can you do for me?
Why should I do business with you?
What makes you different from all the other advisors?

They seem like basic questions, don't they? The problem is that many advisors can't answer them. When I do find advisors who can, most can only do it verbally, and almost none of it is showcased in their printed and online material. Have you heard this before:

> *I'm a financial advisor in [city], [state], [firm], [office]. I help families, individuals, and businesses ensure their financial goals are in line with their personal circumstances. I'm a certified, blah blah blah. I live in [residence], I'm married to [spouse], I have [number] kids, I'm an avid golfer, and I'm actively involved in the community by serving on various boards to include . . .*

What is that? Why do most of the printed or online value propositions sound the same? Why does there seem to be a filter taking those beautiful things you *say* to your prospects—about how you build relationships, how you work with specific families, and how you go three or four generations deep with your clients—seem to disappear from your marketing materials?

Many advisors will tell me, "David, you can't write exactly what you say." That may be true, but I want you to try something for me. State your value proposition right now. Tell me what makes you different from everyone else. Say it, then write it word for word on paper. You'll find that when it's written, it's so much easier to wordsmith. You'll also find that you don't have to change much at all. Believe me, I've had FAs do this over and over again. What I expect you to have when you finish this chapter is a good value proposition that is exactly in line with who you are and what you do, not something you stole from another advisor's Web site because it sounded good.

During every meeting with an advisor, I usually start by looking at the FA's Web site. Why? Because the Web site is usually the marketing piece that is overlooked, unloved, and mostly generic. The problem becomes clear in a study by Ipsos that reveals that *overall, the affluent spend 23.4 hours per week online and among those earning $250,000 and up, the figure rises to 27.4 hours.*

There are many other studies built around affluent people and the time they spend online, and they all say the same thing: affluent people use the Web for research. Don't you think that after a meeting your prospect is going to look you up on the Web? Google you? What will they learn about you? Will they walk away with a good understanding of who you are and why they should do business with you?

I remember the first time I realized I was Googled. I was in Louisville, Kentucky, working one-on-one with a group of advisors. I was sitting with one of their bigger producers, normal conversation, when I mentioned I had a lot of kids. The advisor responded, "I know because you're Catholic." I laughed (because it was funny) and then realized that I hadn't mentioned to him I was Catholic. He was visibly uncomfortable as he realized his verbal mistake. I asked, "How did you find out I was Catholic?" He nervously muttered, "I Googled you before you came."

You Googled me, I thought. I've never even Googled myself, and this guy who I don't know did a search on the Web on my name. I felt violated, which immediately turned into fear, wondering what he found out. Not that I have a seedy past or anything, but you never know what could be floating around in the Internet. That night, I Googled myself for the first time but certainly not the last.

Whatever you do, make sure that people can walk away from the Web, marketing brochure, trifold, bifold, or any fold, with a good understanding of the value you will bring to the relationship. I'm going to make it even easier for you to write.

Your value proposition, marketing statement, whatever you want to call it, doesn't need to be a book. In fact, if it is a book, many people probably won't want to read it. Write just three paragraphs, which are going to be written for the personality types who will be reading them.

First Paragraph
This is for emotional people. They're usually type As who don't have a lot of time to read marketing copy and value propositions but like to make an emotional connection. If you write the first paragraph for this personality type, you have a much greater chance that they will read the information intended for them.

You have virtually no shot at them reading it if it's "lost" somewhere else in the copy. Bring that information to the top, and don't waste your first sentence with the standard "I'm a financial advisor in *blah blah* [office], [city], and [state]." This is your beachfront property; this is your opener, make it good. I once sat with an advisor who wanted the perfect opener for her marketing material. We talked for a while, and I pressed and pressed for what she needed. When we talked about why she was an advisor and what got her into this business she responded with the following:

> *My grandfather told me at a very young age that I would be helping people with their finances because I always had an interest in how money was saved and who was responsible for making sure it's invested properly. I know he's looking down on me today and smiling because I'm doing what I've always wanted to do.*

I yelled, "*That's it!*" That became her opening statement for all her marketing materials. Now, a cynical FA reading this might say that's hokey and cheesy. Well, maybe it is, but it's who she was, and she was okay having people turn away from her business if they didn't like that statement. She honestly didn't want them as clients anyway because she wanted to stay true to herself.

The first paragraph should leave a prospect with a good understanding of how you build relationships over time, how you create a family atmosphere, and go three generations deep with your clients. Let them know you understand their hopes, dreams, and fears. Demonstrate that you are compassionate, listen carefully, and are constantly accessible. This is the paragraph for emotional people, so reach out to them.

Second Paragraph
This is written for the analytical people who, by the way, usually read everything. They are the personality type that goes to a mortgage closing and actually reads all 150 documents. This is the group that after reading the first paragraph will say, "Well, that's very touching, but I want to know *how* you'll get this done. What is your investment philosophy? What certifications do you have? How do you manage risk?" This is where you tell them about your CFP or CHFC or any other certifications you picked up.

One caution about certifications. Many people have them, but very few actually explain to the common person why we should care that they have it. What does CFP mean to me? Why is that a good thing? How does it make you a better advisor? You need to explain all your certifications in regular language and don't just assume that the public is mesmerized by the cool registered mark you have after your title.

Third Paragraph
This is the easiest one. It's where you state how long you've been in the industry, your current company, from what schools you graduated, what degrees you earned, who you're married to, how many children you have, your hobbies, and your community activities.

If you have enough community activities to fill a paragraph, make that paragraph number 3, and the personal info will become paragraph 4. Be very careful with your hobbies because some of them can scare away business. Look at every hobby and decide if there is a negative to it, if someone could be offended by the interest or hobby. And then decide whether or not you care.

I was in the southern United States working with an advisor whose hobby was hunting deer. I said to the advisor, "A prospect could read that and have a problem with you hunting deer. You could lose that prospect." The advisor's response was, "Then I don't want the business." Nothing wrong with that; it's your business, and you get to choose your clients. I just want you to be aware of the possible problems.

Spend time saying your value prop. Do it in the shower, car, bike, and treadmill. In the past, I called this the "elevator speech," just as everyone else did. And then I visited an office on the outskirts of Detroit, where I was working with a group of very young, very new advisors on their elevator speeches. I was role-playing for a while when one of the trainees raised her hand timidly and said, "You know, this is great and all, but we don't really run into prospects on elevators too much." That's the day I stopped using "elevator speech" and started using "value proposition."

Why should I do business with you and what makes you different from everyone else?

Notes

Notes

Notes

Notes

Notes

CHAPTER 8

GIFTS, BIRTHDAYS, HOLIDAYS, AND SPECIAL OCCASIONS

Do you send your clients birthday cards every year? If so, I applaud you. But before patting yourself on the back for being a master relationship builder, consider that your birthday card sits on your clients' desks mixed in with birthday cards from their automobile dealership, accountant, attorney, real estate agent, clothing salespeople, and virtually every other business contact they might have had over the past four or five years.

So you might say, "What's wrong with that? It doesn't diminish me for remembering their birthdays." But don't be so sure. The problem is that you're putting yourself on the same level as all those other people. Do you, for example, have the same relationship with your client as a car salesman? The answer has to be no. You're better than that; your relationship has to be deeper than that, and your responsibility and position in your clients' service hierarchy needs to be number one.

So why are you operating like all the others? Why do you just react to an opportunity to communicate with a client by using a simple card? Are you making a personal call? Are you calling the spouse on his or her birthday? Sending a card? Do you even know when the spouse's birthday is? And finally, with all the data you've gathered over the years, do you go beyond birthdays? What about anniversaries? Children's graduations? New additions to the family? Use the data mining approach from an earlier chapter to go deeper with your clients.

Cards

In the early days at Merrill Lynch, I bled blue, and I admit, I was blinded by the brand rather than offering my own marketing opinions and advice. When my presentation talked about cards—birthday, anniversary, Christmas, Chanukah, sympathy, and others—I would proudly display the branded cards we made available. FAs could order pictures of the famous bull overlooking a small town, complete with snow-covered trees, painting a wonderful Christmas picture. There was a card showing the bull inside a tree ornament. We even had a bull at the base of a menorah for our Chanukah card. Even though I made them available, I thought the cards were inappropriate, but many of my marketing colleagues disagreed with me. Hear me out even if you disagree.

I arrived home one cold December evening and retrieved the mail which was chock-full of Christmas cards. My wife and I went through each and every one with the excitement of children opening presents under the tree. Oh look how big the Johnson baby has gotten. My goodness, the Smith's kids are now teenagers. Look at this funny picture and that funny picture.

I opened a card from a marine friend of mine who was stationed in Iraq. The cover had an illustration of Santa Claus sitting on a tank. I disgustedly threw away the card, much to my wife's surprise. She wasn't particularly impressed with the idea of Santa astride a tank, but she couldn't grasp why it upset me so much. I explained that while I love to brand things with the marine logo, there are some things that shouldn't be juxtaposed because they have absolutely nothing in common. What could be more opposite than Santa—a symbol of holiday cheer—and a tank, which is a killing machine?

That was the moment when it hit me that we were doing the same thing at Merrill Lynch with our iconic bull. If the message is to wish a client or prospect a Merry Christmas, Happy Holiday, Happy Chanukah, Happy Birthday, Happy Anniversary, or to express sorrow over a personal loss, then why do you need the branding? What purpose does it serve? Your clients know who you are and who you work for.

Now, having said that, I *do* think the brand belongs on follow-up note cards to prospects and on any note card you send to a client when discussing business and investments. Note cards should be handwritten and should draw information from your database to ensure there's a personal connection. But keep them simple, clean, and elegant because you're not an insurance salesman; you're the professional who's managing a client's financial future.

I'm often asked what type of holiday cards help differentiate advisors and get their messages through the door. I have no study to quote, but I have a strong opinion. Think about your own holiday ritual; what happens to the standard, branded cards you receive from your CPA, attorney, or real estate agent? For me, and for many to whom I've posed this question, the answer is unanimous: the cards go in the *trash*.

How do you avoid the round file? Some advisors have been successful by creating photo cards. No, I'm not talking about a cheesy shot taken with an iPhone. I'm talking about a professionally taken picture that offers the client a side of the FA not before seen. Maybe the FA and an assistant or a picture of the whole team that serves the client. Maybe a glimpse of the FA's family or even a combination of the two. One idea is to have the picture taken in a historical setting that's mentioned in the narrative on the card. And move to a different location each year, creating a tradition that certainly demonstrates thought and might even build interest.

This is effective because people have a hard time throwing away photo cards. It seems almost sacrilegious. Once I came across a card that had a cute photo with attractive children, but we didn't know the family. We must have received it by mistake, and I put it in the discard pile but was immediately reprimanded by my wife. "What are you doing? Why are you throwing that card away?" I thought it was pretty obvious that since we didn't know the family, there was no reason to keep the card. My wife left no doubt who was in charge of this situation: "David, it's a cute photo, and we can't just throw it in the garbage."

You want to cut through the clutter during the holidays or other events? You want to get the ultimate, long-lasting honor of making it onto your client's refrigerator? Send a professionally crafted photo card. I *know* it works because I've heard the success stories from advisors who do it every year and who are pleased to have clients respond with kind messages about the kids growing up, how nice to see the family in front of a local landmark, you name it.

I've also seen an increase in Thanksgiving cards meant to beat the Christmas and Chanukah onslaught. Personally, I hate them. Happy Thanksgiving? Seriously, why not Happy Groundhog Day? I'm sure there won't be major competition in the mailbox that day, but what's the message? If you want to make a contact, call, but don't send a silly card on the wrong day.

Gifts

This is often an issue for FAs usually because they don't gather data on their clients or don't pay attention to what they have. I'm constantly asked for my opinion on various gifts for clients—especially around the holidays. It usually starts with, "Hey, David, I'm sending my best clients a fruit basket for the holidays. What do you think about that?" Actually, I love fruit baskets, as long as they're accompanied with a card that reads as well as this:

Bob and Mary,

Merry Christmas, we hope you have a wonderful holiday and a very happy New Year. We know your annual holiday party is tomorrow night and thought this fruit basket would make a nice addition to the beautiful dessert table you have every year. We're so sorry we can't make it this year; we are going to particularly miss the homemade apple pie you bake every year. We're always here for you and will be on call throughout the holiday season.

Sincerely,
Your Financial Advisor and Team

The idea is to get personal, to drive home that you know your clients, you know what's going on in their lives, and that your relationship is deep. The only way to do this is based on your data; otherwise, sending a fruit basket is stock, standard, and less effective.

I was with an FA team that had spent north of $5,000 in Christmas wreaths as gifts for their top ninety clients. They were proud of the wreaths and had been sending them for years. I asked how they knew the clients liked the wreaths. They responded emphatically: "They love them! The clients send us e-mails and cards every year, thanking us." I asked how many clients sent "thank you" e-mails and cards to show their appreciation for the expensive wreaths. The answer was thirty clients. I couldn't help but wonder about the other sixty clients: Did they like the wreaths? Love them? Want them? Were they Christian? Nothing was known about the sixty nonresponders.

Think about that for a moment. How many times in your business do you do something you've justified for years because of feedback from just a few clients? You need to question everything you do and find a way to kick it up a notch. In the wreath example, the team wasn't even sure all their recipients were Christian! What a waste of money to send a wreath to a Jewish family. Even worse, might a Jewish family find it offensive that their FA wasn't aware of that piece of personal information?

I left the FA team with a piece of tactical advice. Since most of their clients were local, I told them to select twenty who had never sent positive feedback about the wreath and drive past their homes to see if the wreath was hanging on the front door. That's at least a starting point to determine whether the gift was paying off or not. At the least, for goodness' sake, stop sending the wreath to Jewish families. (Look for menorahs in the window!)

Once again, a gift becomes special when it's accompanied with a note card and a message that says something like this:

> *Bob and Mary,*
>
> *We hope this letter finds you well and want to wish you and all the kids a very merry Christmas and happy New Year. We're sending this wreath to thank you for opening your home to us and inviting us to your family Christmas party last year. Mary mentioned to me that she needed to replace her wreath as the one she's used for so many years was looking weathered.*
>
> *We look forward to serving you for another year and wish you all the best for next year.*
>
> *Sincerely,*
> *Your Financial Advisor and Team*

BAM, that's a contact! It's never about how much the gift costs, especially since we're all aware of SEC regulations around how much you can spend on a client. The gift is about how well you know each and every person in your book and making sure they know that what they are receiving is not stock or standard. Even the most stubborn advisors have trouble arguing about that, but for those who do, I simply ask this question:

> *What did you get your wife for Christmas? Did you get your kids the same thing? Using your model for holiday giving, will you just give the same gift to everyone in your family, knock it out real quick, and be finished with the whole gift-giving thing?*

Think about that because I don't believe gifts are about the cost. And I'm telling you that giving a client a $5 sleeve of golf balls will go a lot further than a $40 bottle of wine *if* the golf balls are accompanied by a note with the following inscription:

Joe,

I know that you go down to Myrtle Beach with your brother to play golf after Christmas. I also know you seem to like hitting balls into the water! Thought you could use a couple of extra balls for the water holes. Hit one in for me.

We'll talk when you get back. Have a great vacation!

Sincerely,
Your Financial Advisor and Team

Does it work or is it all b.s.? Well, try it, and answer that question yourself. I've coached many advisors, and I can tell you that it *does* work; it *does* help you dive deeper, and it *does* help bring in new assets and retain existing assets because it drives home the one thing that clients crave most: *the relationship!*

Notes

Notes

Notes

Notes

CHAPTER 9

THE GIFT TO INSPIRE

Having the ability to inspire people is a gift and an opportunity that can change a person's life. I never understood the full impact until I became a drill instructor.

When I graduated from Marine Corps boot camp, I was an eighteen-year-old youngster who knew very little about life. But I knew one thing that Friday morning: I had accomplished something special. I stood with about three hundred other young marines, facing a crowd of officers, dignitaries, parents, and family members. They were proud of us, and we were proud of ourselves.

I had never worked so hard for something in my life. I did things I never thought I could do: rappel off a fifty-foot tower, go into a tear gas chamber (a real hazing ritual), and run and walk many miles with a heavy pack on my back and weighted boots on my feet. I was exhausted but energized at the same time. I did it, and that sense of accomplishment was earned through and through. When the officer stood before the microphone and addressed us with "Good Morning, Marines," those three words shot through my body like a bolt of lightning. It was intoxicating, and I would try to replicate that feeling for the next nine years.

I had never felt anything like the feeling of accomplishment and satisfaction that came from hard work. During the years following that graduation day, I found success in the Marine Corps through reenlistment ceremonies, promotions, medals of achievement, certificates of achievements, and minor and major things. Each time I prepared myself for all those ceremonies, I thought I'd feel the same euphoria that had embraced me on the parade deck in Parris Island. But each time, I left empty. The feeling wasn't there; it was never there, and it always left me wondering if it would ever return.

Then I went through one of the hardest experiences in the Marine Corps: Marine Drill Instructor School. On the morning of our graduation, I thought I was going to feel it again. I worked hard for my "Smokey the Bear" hat, and when it was presented to me, I was sure I was going to feel that "surge" of electricity. Unfortunately, when I walked across the stage to receive my hat and certificate, my senses were, once again, flat. I just didn't feel it.

The good news is I finally felt the thunderbolt again, and it was completely unexpected and about one hundred times stronger. It was the day I marched my initial group of recruits across the parade deck, called them marines for the first time, and watched their faces flush with accomplishment, sense of direction, confidence, spirit, discipline, and appreciation. It was so powerful, it almost overwhelmed me. I fought to retain my composure as the sensation ran over me like a freight train. And that's when I realized:

> *Your achievements may be great, of that there can be no doubt. But truly great are the achievements of those you lead, inspire, and motivate.*

Go out and inspire your clients and colleagues. You have a huge responsibility and the chance to make a difference in your clients' lives.

See the opportunity and seize it!

ACKNOWLEDGEMENTS

Wow, so many people to thank, so I'll start at the top:

I thank God, my Creator, for always showing me the way and giving me the strength to push forward. You guided me through taking care of two beautiful babies on my own. I was lost but you brought me to St Peter's, you brought me to Sister Mary, you brought me to Father Cellini and you brought me to a community that welcomed me and helped me adjust to this new world and role that changed my life forever. You are my light and my salvation!

To my Beautiful Wife and Children
You are the reason I get up every morning with a smile on my face. Without you, I would be lost.

> To Andy, for putting up with me and loving me unconditionally. You accepted the three of us without any hesitation and sacrificed so much to be a part of our lives. We have now grown, actually we've more than doubled in size; what a life we've built together. You challenge me everyday to be a better person, a person who is closer to God, a person who forgives (still working on that) and a person who does not judge others (working on that, too). You are my spiritual role model and the best Mommy a man could ever be blessed with for his children.

> To Brittany, my first born, the little girl with the cabbage patch cheeks and platinum blonde hair who has grown into a beautiful, smart, accomplished and independent young woman. I'm so proud of you BritBrat!

> To Mikey, you are my boy, you will always be my best friend and I will cherish our baseball trips forever. I could never be more proud of what you have accomplished and who you are

after having been through a couple of extremely tough years. It was all worth it...YOU are so worth it!

To Maddy, my sweet angel, who is always looking out for her daddy, you have the passion, brains and drive to be anything you want to be, no limits, no walls, no barriers.

To Ella, you are the feisty one of the bunch. Your smile and joyful spirit warm my heart! I can't wait to see what you become when you grow up—and I thank God I get a front row seat to the show.

To #5, you are growing in Mommy's belly and all I can say is that your life will not be boring. You will have a lot of hand-me-downs and a huge amount of love surrounding you.

To my Family
You have always been there for me and your support is unwavering. You've been with me in my finest and darkest hours; thank you for never leaving my side. Mom, Dad and Dad, all three of you had a part in molding and mentoring me and I love you all! Randi, Buffi, Tony and Tami, you guys kept me grounded and made sure I was never alone, even in the bathroom. Randi and Buffi, you are more than my sisters, you are my best friends! To my Godmother, you are my spiritual guide and mentor but, most importantly, I thank you and my Godfather for giving life to my wife! Without her, well, I would be alone. To the Jensens, Schneiders and Kennedys, you opened your hearts and doors and welcomed me in. There was never a moment when I felt as if I didn't belong. I love you Aunt Judy; it wasn't the chocolate donuts and chocolate milk that were special, it was that you knew they were my favorites! You will always be my Aunt Juicy!

To my Friends
Thank you for never allowing me to give less than 100 percent. To my best man, Dan, we haven't stayed in touch but you stood by my side through the divorce and then stood by my side at my wedding three years later. You are a great man and a great friend. Charlie, the night we met at Moore's Tavern, that was the push I needed to make this happen. You lit the fire.

To my Marine Brothers and Sisters
Thank you for making me push myself to the limit, which helped me realize there really aren't any limits, we only limit ourselves.

To my Colleagues at Merrill Lynch
You will always have a special place in my heart. You filled a gap that had been missing since I left my beloved Marine Corps. Your passion, energy, motivation, discipline and complete devotion to our mission—the Clients—reminded me of a world I left in 1999. I will never be able to repay you, but know that the four years I spent traveling to over 350 offices in 43 states were incredible. I had the opportunity to meet thousands of you and, with every visit, you opened your doors and welcomed me, no matter in which city or small town I found myself.

A Very Special Thanks
To three people who made this book come to life: my humble writing coach, "N", Shawn Savage of Savage Initiative, my friend and amazing artist who designed the cover and John J. Pacetti, from Timeless Studios, who took the photo's. All of you took a chance on me and worked for peanuts. I couldn't have done it without you!

AUTHOR'S BIOGRAPHY

David joined Merrill Lynch in 1999, and began coaching, training and motivating Financial Advisors for the firm in 2006. He's worked with and presented to well over 10,000 Financial Advisors and is an expert in helping advisors put structure around marketing and relationship building. In 2007, David was honored as one of the inaugural David Brady Award Recipients. This award was created in the honor and name of a beloved Merrill Lynch Financial Advisor who lost his life in the World Trade Center on September 11, 2001. Only eight recipients each year receive this distinguished award throughout the entire Merrill Lynch Company worldwide.

Prior to joining Merrill Lynch, David served his country as a United States Marine for eleven years and finished his service as a Drill Instructor making Marines in Parris Island. David is actively involved in his community and has served on the Zoning and Planning Boards as well as a commissioner for the Parks and Recreation Department. David created an annual event that raises money for wounded veterans called "Freehold Township Day, A Concert and Movie in the Park". For his work in the community, David was honored as the Volunteer of the Year for Monmouth County in 2008.

David and his wife Andrea live in Freehold, NJ with their four children, Brittany, Michael, Madelynn and Ella and are expecting their 5th child in September, 2011.